LOVE'S DELIGHTS

THE JOYS OF MARRIAGE & FAMILY

RICK HOWE

BOOKS BY RICK HOWE

Path of Life: Finding the Joy You've Always Longed For, 2012, University Ministries Press Revised Edition, 2017. 279 pages.

River of Delights: Quenching Your Thirst For Joy, Volume 1, 2015, University Ministries Press Revised Edition, 2017. 230 pages.

River of Delights: Quenching Your Thirst For Joy, Volume 2, 2015, University Ministries Press Revised Edition, 2017. 250 pages.

Living Waters: Daily Refreshment for Joyful Living, 2017, University Ministries Press. 393 pages.

Reasons of the Heart: Joy and the Rationality of Faith, 2017, University Ministries Press. 250 pages.

FOR SMALL GROUP STUDIES

Enjoying God: Discovering the Greatest of All Pleasures, University Ministries Press, 2017. 122 pages.

Love's Delights: The Joys of Marriage and Family, University Ministries Press, 2017. 104 pages.

Sacred Patterns: Work, Rest, and Play in a Joyful Vision of Life, University Ministries Press, 2017. 122 pages.

Kingdom Manifesto: A Call to Joyful Activism, University Ministries Press, 2017. 104 pages.

Joy and the Problem of Evil, University Ministries Press, Boulder, 2017. 122 pages.

For more information, visit www.rickhowe.org.

UNIVERSITY MINISTRIES PRESS
BOULDER, COLORADO
Copyright © 2015.
University Ministries Press Edition, 2017.

This book represents five chapters from Rick Howe, *Rivers of Delight: Quenching Your Thirst For Joy, Volume 1* (Boulder, CO: University Ministries Press, Revised Edition, 2017). Used by Permission.

ISBN: 978-0-9962696-5-0

ABBREVIATIONS

NIV   New International Version
RSV   Revised Standard Version

CONTENTS

AUTHOR'S NOTE

The material in *Love's Delights* is taken from my work, *River of Delights: Quenching Your Thirst For Joy, Volume 1.* I thought it would be worthwhile to take a major section of that book and make a "mini-book" for readers who wish to explore this very important topic on its own.

As you will see, there are many endnotes. If texts of Scripture are not given in full in the main body of a chapter, they have been included in the endnotes to make it possible for you to read the book without the extra chore of looking them up yourself. There are also many references to other works, as well as my own comments. My suggestion is that you read *Love's Delights* first without interacting with the endnotes to trace the flow of thought without interruption, and then read it again with those references.

The "Questions for Thought and Discussion" for each chapter reflect my hope that you will study this book with others, my belief that learning in community is the best way to learn, and my prayer that God will use this book to create communities of joy for the advancement of his Kingdom.

PREFACE

An apocalyptic foreboding has many in its grip, strengthened by endless newsfeeds and broadcasts featuring economic woes, violence, terrorism, wars and threats of war, corruption in high places, depletion of energy resources, global climate change, natural catastrophes, pestilence, and toxins in our environment and our food.

No wonder words like *anxiety*, *depression*, *melancholy*, and *stress* are used to describe our generation! Historians in the future might well call ours *The Age of Prozac*. Depressive disorders are widespread. The pharmaceutical industry has grown rich on them.

The fact that this emotional epidemic grows unabated should signal the possibility that we have misdiagnosed and mistreated the problem. I don't deny that there are frightening factors behind our personal angst and cultural malaise, but I believe that there is an underlying cause that we ignore at our own greater peril. We are disoriented and dysfunctional. We are disoriented because we have removed God from our vision of life, and dysfunctional because we vainly attempt to live without him. Much else (economic woes, violence, toxins in our environment, et al) results directly or indirectly from this.

"A joyful heart is a good medicine."[1] This was once proverbial wisdom. It is true because joy connects us with God, and that is the healthiest place for us to be. Dallas Willard wrote, "Full joy is our first line of defense against weakness, failure, and disease of mind and body."[2] Peter Kreeft says much the same: "A joyful spirit inspires joyful feelings and even a more psychosomatically healthy body. (For example, we need less sleep when we have joy and have more resistance to all kinds of diseases from colds to cancers.)"[3] This ancient wisdom deserves a revival in our day. In fact, it is our only hope.

The premises of this book are that joy links us with God, it can touch and transform every dimension of our lives, including our marriage and family relationships, and we will flourish only as we position ourselves to receive this gift from Him. Read on to discover how!

CHAPTER 1

EDEN'S JOY

If there is an institution endangered in our day, it is marriage and family. Though it would be worth exploring, I will leave to others how this factors into the demise of our culture. My concern here is the loss of joy that inevitably attends the weakening and destruction of these relationships. Tear the fabric, destroy the joy in its delicate weave. My interest is revisiting ancient insights into marriage and family as a foundation for human flourishing, and persuading as many as possible that there is great joy to be found here!

There is no better place to begin our exploration than the teaching of Jesus. When he was asked to give his views on marriage, his starting point was not later chapters in the human narrative that show this relationship in its fallenness and sin, but the very first chapter of our story, where we see God's intention and design unmarred by our failings.[1] This is what he said:

> Have you not read that he who created them from the beginning made them male and female, and said, 'Therefore a man shall leave his father and his mother and hold fast to his wife, and the two shall become one flesh'? So they are no longer two but one flesh.

What therefore God has joined together, let not man separate. (Matthew 19:4-6)

Because of your hardness of heart Moses allowed you to divorce your wives, but from the beginning it was not so. (Matthew 19:8)

At his word, we will begin with the opening lines of the human story.

MARRIAGE AND THE IMAGE OF GOD

When was the last time you attended a wedding ceremony that celebrated marriage as a display of God's image in humanity? Not sure you can think of any? Yet that is what this relationship is meant to be:

Then God said, "Let us make mankind in our image, in our likeness, so that they may rule over the fish in the sea and the birds in the sky, over the livestock and all the wild animals, and over all the creatures that move along the ground."

So God created mankind in his own image,
  in the image of God he created them;
  male and female he created them. (Genesis 1:26-27, NIV)

To say that God is a Trinity is to affirm that the one God is a community of Persons – Father, Son, and Holy Spirit – who delight in each other and revel in the beatitude of their shared love.[2] To say that we were created in the image of this God – which is the first thing we learn about ourselves in the sacred Scriptures – is to say that we were made to mirror God in finite, embodied ways in the world he created. It is not our design, but the Creator's. Our understanding of marriage must begin here.

In the opening chapter of the human story we discover that Adam-alone was not Adam-complete. Following a series of benedictions, "And God saw that it was good,"[3] we find this exception: "Then the LORD God said, 'It is not good that the man should be alone.'"[4] Why? Because we were made to live in community. We are fulfilled and find our identity in life shared with others. While humans-as-such bear the image of God ("In the image of God he created them."), it is in relationships, and especially in our gendered relationships as men and women and as husbands and wives, that we bear the image of God together ("Male and female he created them.").[5] This is fundamental to our humanity, and essential to the good and wise intentions of our Creator. It is foundational to God's plan for marriage.[6]

The story develops:

> Then the LORD God said, "It is not good that the man should be alone; I will make him a helper fit for him." Now out of the ground the LORD God had formed every beast of the field and every bird of the heavens and brought them to the man to see what he would call them. And whatever the man called every living creature, that was its name. The man gave names to all livestock and to the birds of the heavens and to every beast of the field. But for Adam there was not found a helper fit for him. So the LORD God caused a deep sleep to fall upon the man, and while he slept took one of his ribs and closed up the place with flesh. And the rib that the LORD God had taken from the man he made into a woman and brought her to the man. Then the man said,
>
> > "This at last is bone of my bones
> > and flesh of my flesh;
> > > she shall be called Woman,
> > because she was taken out of Man." (Genesis 2:18-23)

In the inspired narrative of our beginnings Adam was in the Garden with the animals he named. As he watched creatures in gendered pairs, he knew that someone was missing from his life. One day he awoke from a deep sleep to discover that the Creator had brought another to him – like him,[7] and yet different from him in ways that caught the breath in his throat, quickened the beat of his heart, rushed the blood through his veins, and stirred new and powerful emotions and desires within him. When he beheld this new creation in her unclothed feminine splendor, the exclamation of astonished delight leapt from his lips: "This at last is bone of my bones and flesh of my flesh!"

From that moment on, Eden held pristine possibilities for the first couple, fully envisioned by the Creator and yet to be discovered by them. In body and soul they would share an intimacy of life, love, and joy that mirrored the life, love, and joy of the Triune God who made them.

TWO BECOME ONE

There is an infinite chasm between God and everything else. He is incomparable. *Sui generis.* Yet his Word also tells us that he created humans in his image. There is an analogy between God and us, designed and disclosed by the Creator himself.[8] This not only enables us to think and talk meaningfully about God, it helps us understand who we are and the task he has given to us as his image-bearers. This illumines the creation story, retold in the words of Jesus:

> [Jesus] answered, "Have you not read that he who created them from the beginning made them male and female, and said, 'Therefore a man shall leave his father and his mother and hold fast to his wife, and the two shall become one flesh'? So they are no

longer two but one flesh. What therefore God has joined together, let not man separate." (Matthew 19:4-6)

Although he might have chosen another way, in his creative wisdom the Triune God crafted a finite, embodied reflection of his oneness in the unity ("one flesh") and life-long commitment ("What therefore God has joined together, let not man separate.") of a man and woman ("he . . . made them male and female").[9] Together-as-one-for-a-lifetime.[10] The union of husband and wife in the covenant of marriage is a sign that points to a higher, greater, spiritual reality. Their gendered unity offers a faint glimpse of the eternal union of the Triune God in human experience.[11]

Like their Triune Maker, Adam and Eve formed a communion of equals. Equal in their participation in the image of God, and evenly matched in the dignity of that status. Their bond of mutual love and shared joy would not have been possible otherwise. Adam didn't need a lesser being to share life with. He needed someone who, with him, would bear the image of God. He needed someone whom he could describe with the words "bone of my bone and flesh of my flesh." Neither one greater, neither lesser.[12]

Like the Persons of the Trinity, Adam and Eve were equal and yet wonderfully different. Their oneness did not negate their differences, but made them complementary, each enhancing and enriching the other, together singing in harmony, dancing in step across the Garden floor. The contours and capacities of their bodies were a perfect fit. Their nuanced masculine and feminine gifts created possibilities together that neither had apart from the other. Only Adam could pleasure Eve and contribute to the wonder of fruitfulness that made her "the mother of all living."[13] Only Eve could pleasure Adam and through their shared delight make him a father of children and the representative of all mankind.[14] As they ventured into life together, only Adam could husband Eve.[15] Only Eve could help Adam.[16] Their pleasure lay in delighting in their differences, and through them, becoming one. One in life. One for a lifetime. Masculine and feminine in a joyful embrace, fulfilling the call to bear God's image in the world.

NAKED AND UNASHAMED

In their union Adam and Eve *knew* each other.[17] This is not a euphemism for people who feel uncomfortable talking about sex. It is a positive description of intimacy and transparency, disclosure and discovery, between a man and woman in which they give themselves fully to each other. "And the man and his wife were both naked and were not ashamed."[18]

In the Garden Adam and Eve would not have known what privacy was or why one would want or need it. If you had told them that nudity in their relationship should be veiled, you would have seen confusion in their eyes and heard loud guffaws of incredulity in response. There was nothing to hide. There were no secrets. There was no vulnerability. No need to protect oneself from the other. In time Adam and Eve in the Garden would have come to know as much as they could about each other, and would have delighted in every detail.

Adam was welcomed and embraced by Eve as God's gift to her. He entrusted himself fully to her. Eve was genuinely impressed with Adam's manliness, and knew that this pleased him greatly. There were only words of admiration and generous approval, spoken truly from her heart, in praise of his masculine form. He was handsome and strong in her eyes, and that was the only mirror he had. That is how he saw himself. There was no need to be brash, because he knew that he was fully desirable to his wife as he was. There was no need to hide what made him so obviously different from Eve. Modesty had no meaning and served no purpose. He enjoyed pleasing Eve with his body, delighting in the knowledge that giving himself fully to her enriched and fulfilled her sexuality in the Creator's good and wise design.[19]

Eve was welcomed and embraced by Adam as God's gift to him. She entrusted herself fully to him. There were only words of appreciation and affirmation, spoken truly from his heart, in praise of her feminine form. She was beautiful in his eyes, and that was the only mirror she had. That is how she saw herself. There was no need to flaunt her features, because she knew that she was fully desirable to her husband as she was. There was no need to be demure. Modesty had no meaning and served no purpose. She enjoyed pleasing Adam with her body, delighting in the knowledge that giving herself fully to him enriched and fulfilled his sexuality in the Creator's good and wise design.[20]

FRUITFULNESS

In their innocence Adam and Eve were neither takers nor misers. Each was a generous giver and an enjoyable gift. They delighted in giving and receiving pleasure, loving and being loved, knowing that this reflected something of the love and joy of their Creator. Their masculine and feminine bodies enabled them to express their love to each other in ways that were unique to each and a pleasure to both. They experienced sexual pleasure as the beatitude of their shared love, and couldn't have imagined it any other way. This was the heart of the fruitfulness God had in store for them.

"And God blessed them. And God said to them, 'Be fruitful and multiply and fill the earth.'"[21] In these ancient words some see a moral obligation for married couples, if possible, to have children. Roman Catholics see procreation as a dictate of natural law. (If we let nature take its course in sexual relations, children are usually the result. It is nature's law, and therefore the Maker's law.) Protestants have often seen this text as a command to be obeyed.

Let me propose, instead, that these words are a blessing that results in the gift of children. Commands are to be obeyed; blessings are to be treasured and enjoyed.[22] Procreation is not a duty; children are not an obligation. It is all an expression of God's favor to enable us to flourish in life. It is meant for our joy. It makes a difference. A big difference![23]

If you find yourself unfamiliar or even uncomfortable with this, let me give you three reasons for considering it. First, why would Adam and Eve need a command to have sex (the only way to be fruitful and multiply)? I never had to command my children to eat their favorite food or play their favorite game. Second, if being sexually fruitful and having children is a moral imperative given to humans-as-such, then Jesus failed.[24] Really? Third, these very words were used of the animal kingdom earlier in the same chapter: "And God blessed them, saying, "Be fruitful and multiply and fill the waters in the seas, and let birds multiply on the earth."[25] Do fish and birds have the capacity to fulfill moral obligations? I don't think so, but the language is the same.

No, something else is happening here. This is the language of blessing. (How could we miss this when the words "Be fruitful and multiply" are prefaced with the words "And God blessed them"?) In the ancient Scriptures God blesses people, animals, land, dwelling places, crops and other things.[26] His blessing is an endowment of power. When God speaks in blessing, his word brings about the intentions of his heart. His blessings not only display his great might, they bestow his favor, and reflect his goodness and generosity toward his creatures.[27] This puts us in a better position to understand the text in Genesis 1. The marriage relationship is a blessing from God.[28] Sexual pleasure shared by a husband and wife is his blessing.[29] God created us in a way that we would, in fact, pursue this.[30] The mystery and wonder of conception, and the unseen growth of new human life in a mother's womb, are further blessings from our Creator. Children are a bonus from his good hand. They exhibit God's creative power and are meant for our joy.[31]

The primal blessing of marital fruitfulness plays two roles in fulfilling God's plan for our planet. It is integral to Creation and Redemption. Through the bearing and rearing of children we are enabled to fulfill the mandate to harness and steward the resources of the earth, and to marshal our God-given creativity for his glory and our good.[32] It is also through marriage and the gift of children, generation after generation, that God would one day bring his Son into the world as an infant, who would grow to be a man, to bring redemption to it.[33]

ORIGINAL JOY

Theologians have much to say about what they call *original sin*. It refers not only to the sin of our first parents, but the solidarity of the human race in that sin. It is crucial to our understanding not only of the human condition in Adam, but to our understanding of redemption, and the status of the redeemed in Christ. Too little attention is given to *original joy*.[34] For a time it bound all of creation together. It was the nexus of our relationships with each other and with God, and a mirror of God's Triune joy on the earth.[35] Marriage is meant for our joy. Family life is meant to multiply it, filling the earth with children who will become husbands, wives, and parents, creating an ever-expanding joy in our Maker and a shared joy in all that he has made. Do you not long for this? Does it not beckon you?

QUESTIONS FOR THOUGHT AND DISCUSSION

1. How does this chapter's discussion of the image of God help you understand the Trinity? And how does this understanding of the Trinity influence your view of marriage?

2. "And the man and his wife were both naked and were not ashamed." What does this imply about their relationship? What kind of relationship would have to be the case for this to be true?

3. How does the phrase "equal, wonderfully different, and complementary" illumine the Trinity and your understanding of male and female in a marriage relationship? How does this differ from other relational models that are advocated in our society or in the Church?

4. Do you see the words, "Be fruitful and multiply" as a command to be obeyed? What difference would it make to see this not as command, but a blessing? How might this impact the problems of unwanted or undervalued children in our society?

5. Have you seen Eden in marriages you know of? What impresses you about these couples? What do you see in them that you want for yourself?

CHAPTER 2

FAR AS THE CURSE IS FOUND

The Fall has taken a terrible toll on our kind. Ripples from the primal stone thrown into the pond of humanity have reached shore all the way around. We may think that our fallen condition is normal because we are used to living with it, but it is far, far from that. Marriage and family, the most foundational and formative relationships we have, are mutant. Misshapen. Dysfunctional. It is our own doing, and now it is our undoing.

The garment of marriage and family is in tatters. We have witnessed the unraveling of its seams in our day. Many see marriage as a dispensable (or at least pliable) convention. Fewer marry. Many wait longer to marry. Half who marry, divorce. Many go to great lengths to limit childbearing. Couples who could have children choose not to. Parents pay others to care for their children while they seek to fulfill personal aspirations.

Sex has been ripped from its sacred origins, stripped of its essential meaning, and torn from the context of marriage. We have sown the wind are reaping a whirlwind![1] The land is now strewn with casual sexual liaisons, prolific pornography, sexual perversion and violence, domestic abandonment and abuse, abortion, and infanticide.[2] Broken marriages, broken families, and broken people lie in the wreckage. The tale of tragedy began here:

> The LORD God took the man and put him in the garden of Eden to work it and keep it. And the LORD God commanded the man, saying, "You may surely eat of every tree of the garden, but of the tree of the knowledge of good and evil you shall not eat, for in the day that you eat of it you shall surely die."

> The woman . . . took of its fruit and ate, and she also gave some to her husband who was with her, and he ate. Then the eyes of both were opened, and they knew that they were naked, and they sewed fig leaves together and made themselves loincloths.

> To the woman [the LORD God] said,

> "I will surely multiply your pain in childbearing;
>   in pain you shall bring forth children.
> Your desire shall be for your husband,
>   and she shall rule over you."

> And to Adam he said,

> "Because you have listened to the voice of your wife
>   and have eaten of the tree
> of which I commanded you,
>   'You shall not eat of it,'
> cursed is the ground because of you;
>   in pain you shall eat of it all the days of your life;
> thorns and thistles it shall bring forth for you;
>   and you shall eat the plants of the field.
> By the sweat of your face you shall eat bread,
>   till you return to the ground,

for out of it you were taken;
for you are dust,
and to dust you will return. (Genesis 2:15-17; 3:6-8, 16-19)

The world changed that day. It pivoted and moved in a different and dire direction. Adam and Eve hid from God and then from each other. Sin brought guilt. Guilt brought shame. Shame became the mirror in which they saw themselves. Intimacy and harmony gave way to distance and dissonance. Memories of their pristine love and joy grew dimmer by the day. Affirmation and affection were lost to criticism and blame. The delicate balance of gendered equality and difference became a tug-of-war and sometimes all-out-war, between the sexes. The joys of sexual love gave way to the perverted pleasures of lust. Sibling rivalry and murder followed in the wake.

Woe to us! Eden was such a short chapter in our story; the Fall so lurid and long. The image of God, once our treasured status and the centerpiece of marriage, shuffles like a beggar in dirty rags through trashed alleys of our own making.

NO MORE LET SIN NOR SORROWS GROW!

Imagine the damage of the Fall undone! If you know the Christmas carol *Joy to the World*, feel free to sing this verse:

No more let sin nor sorrows grow,
nor thorns infest the ground.
He comes to make his blessings flow
far as the curse is found.[3]

Many Christians are quick to affirm God's grace as a preparation for heaven, but are not as swift to see the possibilities of grace on the earth in the present.

Yet this is where the Curse is found. This is exactly where God intends to see his blessings flow. This is where he purposes to change factors in the human equation that sum to sorrow's rule.[4]

Starting with Jesus. In the last chapter we saw that when Jesus taught about marriage he refused to take his cues from this relationship in its fallen state, or even from the Scriptures that accommodate our hardness of heart. His standard was nothing less than God's original design in creation. For Jesus, the beginning is still binding. Eden is still God's intention and desire for men and women who enter marriage. Let's read these words again:

> Have you not read that he who created them from the beginning made them male and female, and said, 'Therefore a man shall leave his father and his mother and hold fast to his wife, and the two shall become one flesh'? So they are no longer two but one flesh. What therefore God has joined together, let not man separate. (Matthew 19:4-6)

> Because of your hardness of heart Moses allowed you to divorce your wives, but from the beginning it was not so. (Matthew 19:8)

I understand that following Jesus in pursuit of Eden makes me vulnerable to the charge of impossible idealism. I won't concede the point. If Jesus had been a shrewd politician he would have stepped back from his controversial statement in order to appease opponents and gain supporters.[5] He wasn't; he didn't; nor will I. Because I have fallen short of God's design doesn't mean that I shouldn't pursue it or point others to it. If I fail, it doesn't mean that you should not make the attempt.[6]

The disciples of Jesus responded to his teaching on marriage and its high standards with the despairing comment that it would surely be better not to marry.[7] Jesus knew the high divorce rate in first century Jewish culture.[8] He knew that Moses had permitted divorce.[9] But he also knew that there is an importance difference between accommodation and aspiration: God's accommodation to our sinful condition and his aspiration for us. If they had understood him, his disciples would have responded, "If the hardness of our hearts keeps us from God's desire for our lives, may they become soft and malleable in his hands!" The quality of your marriage and family life begins here. What will become of them, what is possible or impossible for them, starts here.

Understanding ideals. Part of our problem may be a misunderstanding. An ideal is impossible only if we think of it as all or nothing. If it is, our hands will be forever empty. But that isn't the nature of ideals. They are optimal qualities. They represent life at its best. We don't arrive at them; we move toward them. We stay on the path that leads us to them, or wander from it and lose sight of them. Ideals make demands of us, like intentionality, the formation of habits, customs, and long-term commitments; they do not, however, demand perfection in the pursuit. If we understand God's design for marriage as an ideal for us to pursue, we can see how it is possible to say "Yes" to Jesus and follow him, even if more of the path lies before us than behind.

Innocence and the possibilities of grace. We must make a distinction between these two things. The ship of innocence sailed long ago and left us behind. But God hasn't! His grace offered and given to us through Christ creates possibilities that would otherwise be entirely beyond our reach. It can re-create God's original design for marriages and families. It can restore the hearts of husbands and wives, parents and children, and brothers and sisters. Grace can do what we would bet our life savings against if it were up to us, because it is the loving action of the One who is with us, in us, and has all power at his beck and call.

In the same chapter of Matthew's Gospel in which Jesus taught God's ideal for marriage (and received a skeptical response), he pointed to the peril of riches and our need to release them from our grip (and again met with a skeptical response). His words apply to both: "With man this is impossible, but with God all things are possible."[10] Do you believe this? If you don't, you will walk a path of certain disappointment. If you do, the path will open onto vistas you cannot yet see that will take your breath away![11]

Marriage as a reflection. What was given in Creation and lost in the Fall God intends to restore in Redemption. All that was meant for our kind in Eden God intends to make possible for us wherever we make our home. At its heart, this is about the image of God and our calling to reflect the Creator in our lives. As grace renews the image of God in us, smudges and distortions are removed from the reflection. Integrity and wholeness are restored. Health begins and grows. As we are transformed, our life-long commitment to each other in marriage mirrors the eternal union of the Trinity. Our love for each other – the bond of marriage – pictures the bond of love between the Father, Son and Holy Spirit. [12] Our growing joy in each other reflects the overflowing joy of our Triune God.

The primal calling in marriage is still our primary calling. There is more to marriage than this, but not less. There is more to this relationship than meets the eye, but what can be seen is meant to direct attention to the God who made us in ways that honor him. Our understanding of marriage must begin here.

Marriage as a sacred covenant. Our culture sees marriage as a social contract, with terms, conditions, provisions, and rights. If this is what marriage is, any contract will do. Just fill in the blanks with the names of the consenting parties and let them negotiate the stipulations. The disagreement in our day is whether the participants must be male and female, or may also be the same gender.[13]

In a Christian vision of life, marriage in its intended and most robust sense is not a civil union but holy matrimony. A sacred covenant. It is sacred not only because of its divine origin and purpose,[14] and its blessing by Christ,[15] but because its members are three: a man, a woman, and Christ. Its covenant is a pledge of faithful love between a husband, a wife, and the Lord of their marriage.

Marriage is meant to mirror Christ and his relationship with the Church. In the words of the apostle Paul:

> Be filled with the Spirit, addressing one another in psalms and hymns and spiritual songs, singing and making melody to the Lord with your heart, giving thanks always and for everything to God the Father in the name of our Lord Jesus Christ, submitting to one another out of reverence for Christ. (Ephesians 5:18-21)

> Wives, submit to your own husbands, as to the Lord. For the husband is the head of the wife even as Christ is the head of the church, his body, and is himself its Savior. Now as the church submits to Christ, so also wives should submit in everything to their husbands. (Ephesians 5:22-24)

> Husbands, love your wives, as Christ loved the church and gave himself up for her, that he might sanctify her by the washing of water with the word, so that he might present the church to himself in splendor, without spot or wrinkle or any such thing, that she might be holy and without blemish. (Ephesians 5:25-27)

Christ is not a third party in the sacred covenant of marriage, but the first. He does not join us. We join him. He is not an addition to marriage. He is first in rank and relationship. Husbands see Christ first, in reverence honor him, then see and honor their wives through him. Wives see Christ first, in reverence honor him, then see and honor their husbands through him. This is not mere symbolism. It is meant to shape all facets of married life. Everything is to be included; nothing left out.

In a beautifully nuanced mutual submission,[16] a husband is called to give himself in preferential love to his wife, and a wife is called to give herself in deferential love to her husband.[17] Lover and beloved bow before each other. Each honors the other. Each seeks the good of the other and does this joyfully: "singing and making melody to the Lord." Each offers a self-giving love, and seeks to out-give the other. Neither does this with merit in view; both do this from their reverence for Christ.

The bond of the marriage covenant is not merely between a husband and a wife, but between lover, beloved, and the One who loves them both, loved them first, and loves them best. There is great joy in seeing your marriage mirror the love relationship between Christ and his Church. Jonathan Edwards wrote:

> The mutual joy of Christ and his church is like that of bridegroom and bride, in that they rejoice in each other, as those whom they have chosen above others, for their nearest, most intimate, and everlasting friends and companions.
>
> Christ and his church, like the bridegroom and bride, rejoice in each other, as those that are the objects of each other's most tender and ardent love. . . . [Christ] loved the church, and gave himself for it; and his love to her proved stronger than death.

And on the other hand, she loves him with a supreme affection; nothing stands in competition with him in her heart: she loves him with all her heart. Her whole soul is offered up to him in the flame of love.

Christ and his church rejoice in each other's beauty.

Christ and his church, as the bridegroom and bride, rejoice in each other's love.

Christ and his church rejoice in communion with each other, as in being united in their happiness, and having fellowship and a joint participation in each other's good: as the bridegroom and bride rejoice together at the wedding-feast, and as thenceforward they are joint partakers of each other's comforts and joys. [18]

Marriage and sacrament. A sacrament is a sign of the sacred among us. It points beyond itself to a transcendent reality. Baptism and the Lord's Supper are two examples.[19] A sacrament points us to Christ in our midst. When marriage is a sacred covenant between a husband, a wife, and their Lord, it becomes sacramental. It is a token of the gracious presence of Christ: "'Therefore a man shall leave his father and mother and hold fast to his wife, and the two shall become one flesh.' This mystery is profound, and I am saying that it refers to Christ and the church."[20] (Ephesians 5:32) When this truth is embraced and lived, there is nothing ordinary about marriage. Everything a couple does in their relationship can celebrate the presence of Christ and point others to him. Their shared joy becomes a dance that others watch and want to join.

QUESTIONS FOR THOUGHT AND DISCUSSION

1. Discuss the breakdown of marriage and family as you see it in our day. Even in their fallenness, how can marriage and family contribute to human health and wellbeing?

2. Read Matthew 19:4-10, and then this quote from the chapter: Jesus' "standard was nothing less than God's original design in creation. For Jesus, the beginning is still binding. Eden is still God's intention and desire for men and women who enter marriage." How is Jesus' view of marriage different from what you see in our culture and often in the Church?

3. How does an understanding of ideals help your approach marriage and family life?

4. What is the difference between marriage as a sacred covenant and a social contract? What difference does it make?

5. What do you think of the discussion of the nuanced mutual submission of husbands and wives under Christ? Is it true to the Scriptures? Is it true to what you know about Christ?

CHAPTER 3

EDEN AND MORE!

Marriage and family as vocation. When you see the word "vocation," work probably comes first to your mind. In a Christian vision of life, however, vocation is much more than this. It encompasses every dimension of life, including marriage and family. After giving instructions on marriage and singleness to the church in Corinth, the apostle Paul wrote: "Only, as the Lord has assigned to each one, as God has called each, in this manner let him walk. And so I direct in all the churches."[1] Marriage and family are not only institutions ordained by God; they are callings. [2] Vocations. A married man is not a husband because he was declared to be so in a wedding ceremony. He is called by God to be a husband. A married woman is not a wife because she agreed to be so on the day of her wedding. She is called by God to be a wife. Children aren't children simply because they were born to a mother and a father. They are called by God to be children.

Martin Luther wrote:

> Likewise, those who are fathers or mothers, who rule their households well and who beget children for the service of God are

also in a truly holy estate, doing a holy work, and members of a holy order. In the same way when children . . . are obedient to their parents . . . this also is true holiness and those living in such estate are true saints on earth.[3]

It looks like a great thing when a monk renounces everything and goes into a cloister, carries on a life of asceticism, fasts, watches, prays, etc. . . . On the other hand, it looks like a small thing when a maid cooks and cleans and does other housework. But because God's command is there, even such a small work must be praised as a service to God far surpassing the holiness and asceticism of all monks and nuns. . . . there God's command is fulfilled, that one should honour father and mother and help in the care of the home.[4]

God has given this walk of life, fatherhood and motherhood, a special position of honor, higher than that of any other walk of life under it. Not only has he commanded us to love parents but to honor them. In regard to brothers, sisters, and neighbors in general he commands nothing higher than that we love them. But he distinguishes father and mother above all other persons on earth, and places them next to himself. For it is a much higher thing to honor than to love. Honor includes not only love, but also deference, humility, and modesty directed (so to speak) toward a majesty concealed within them. Honor requires us not only to address them affectionately and with high esteem, but above all to show by our actions, both of heart and body, that we respect them very highly and that next to God we give them the very highest place. For anyone whom we are wholeheartedly to honor, we must truly regard as high and great.[5]

If we could listen to the heart-talk of family members who understand the true nature of their relationships, this is what we would hear as they rise for a new day: "I am called this day to be a husband to my wife." "I am called this day to be a wife to my husband." "Lord, give us strength today to fulfill our calling as parents." "Help me fulfill the charge you have given me to honor my mother and father, and to love my brother and sister." We would see a prayerful purpose to fulfill these vocations in the events and tasks of the day.

Husbands are called to give themselves to their wives in sacrificial love and preferential care.[6] Wives are called to give themselves to their husbands in loving respect and deferential care. Together, parents are called to play a prophetic role in the lives of their children, speaking the Word of God into their lives; a priestly role in praying for their children and representing God to them; a protective role, sheltering them as they can from the dangers of the world; and a provisioning role, whether it is daily nurture, or the material goods that are necessary for life. There is great joy in fulfilling these callings from God!

Hallowed be this house![7] Marriage and family relationships are sacred. They are holy. Read with care these words from the apostle Paul:

> To the rest I say (I, not the Lord) that if any brother has a wife who is an unbeliever, and she consents to live with him, he should not divorce her. If any woman has a husband who is an unbeliever, and he consents to live with her, she should not divorce him. For the unbelieving husband is made holy because of his wife, and the unbelieving wife is made holy because of her husband. Otherwise your children would be unclean, but as it is, they are holy. (1 Corinthians 7:12-14)[8]

One Christ-follower in a marriage and family hallows these relationships. The presence of Christ in one makes a difference for all. Our Lord can accomplish much with little! Wherever there is faith in Christ, marriages and families are made holy, set apart by the presence of God and set apart for the purposes of God. This doesn't make them perfect or sinless (so there is no need to pretend that they are). God declares them holy on the basis of faith in Christ, and acts through them to bring about his purposes for the world.

The apostle Paul wrote to Timothy that marriage is good because it is the gift of a good God. He went on to say: "For everything created by God is good, and nothing is to be rejected if it is received with thanksgiving" by those who "believe and know the truth," for it is "made holy by the word of God and prayer."[9] God is holy. Temples are holy. Sacraments are holy. Angels are holy. We are accustomed to these associations. But marriage and family life? Not these relationships in the abstract, but in real life, everyday life, under the same roof? Meals at a table? Children at play? Cleaning the house? Mowing the lawn? This is God's Word, not mine: As his Word shapes our life together, and our prayers consecrate these relationships to his purposes, they are hallowed. All that they involve in day-to-day, feet-on-the-ground life becomes holy. They are set apart from the world and its sinful ways, and set apart for God and his purposes for the world.

Deo Gloria. For what are marriage and family set apart? They exist for the glory of God. It isn't that they do and other dimensions of life don't. All of life is meant for the glory of God, including marriage and family. Luther wrote of marriage:

> [God] wishes us to honor, maintain, and cherish it as a divine and blessed walk of life. He has established it before all others as the first of all institutions, and he created man and woman differently (as is evident) not for indecency but to be true to each other, to be fruitful, to beget children, and to nurture and bring them up to the glory of God. God has therefore blessed this walk of life most richly, above all others, and, in addition, has supplied and endowed it with everything in the world in order that this walk of life might be richly provided for. Married life is no matter for jest or idle

curiosity, but it is a glorious institution and an object of God's serious concern.[10]

To affirm this for your marriage and your family is to embrace something truly wonderful: In these relationships you are caught up in something far greater than the little group that bears a family name and shares life beneath the same roof. The "something greater" is God himself, his purposes for this world, and his honor in it. Your relationships exist to mirror truths about God and his ways. They are meant to point others to him.

Everything created by God can serve his glory. This includes marriage and family life in its day-to-day activities. It has been said of Luther: "[His] faith was simple enough to trust that after a conscientious day's labor, a Christian father could come home and eat his sausage, play his flute, sing with his children, and make love to his wife — all to the glory of God!"[11] If we are unfamiliar and uncomfortable with this robust vision of life made holy by God and devoted to his glory, it signals how far we have wandered from very important truths, how narrow our vision and how blinkered our spiritual eyes have become, and how lamentable we have made ourselves as a result. God wants so much more for us! The One for whom all things are possible can make this possible for your marriage, your family, your life.

COMMON GRACE FOR THE COMMON GOOD

The darkness of our world is pierced by shafts of light. The darkness is ours; the light is God's. He refuses to turn from us in our sin and shame, relentlessly pursues us, and seeks to woo us back to him and the joy of his redemptive love. In his mercy, God spares us the full impact of our rebellion against him. More than we know, he shields us from the growing and deepening evil in the world.[12] There are restraints within us (conscience) and around us (authority) for our protection.[13]   In his grace God gives good things to remind us that he still would see us flourish under his hand. He gives many blessings and provisions to support and enrich our existence – not least of which are people providentially placed in our lives to nurture and care for us.   Husbands and wives.   Mothers and fathers. Sisters and brothers. Aunts, uncles, and cousins. Grandparents. God intends them for our good.

In this chapter of our human story, all marriages and families miss the mark of God's intentions for them. Some more than others. Nevertheless, we should think of them when we read Scriptures like these:

> The LORD is good to all,
> And his mercy is over all that he has made (Psalm 145:9)

> He makes his sun rise on the evil and on the good, and sends rain on the just and on the unjust. (Matthew 5:45)

> God's kindness is meant to lead you to repentance. (Romans 2:4)

> In past generations [God] allowed all the nations to walk in their own ways. Yet he did not leave himself without witness, for he did good by giving you rains from heaven and fruitful seasons, satisfying your hearts with food and gladness. (Acts 14:17)

Marriage and family are tokens of God's commitment to our well-being.[14] Even if God is not honored and thanked for his gifts, he gives them. Many enjoy them.   The world benefits from them.   Even if marriages and families wander from the path that God laid out for them, the world is a better place because of them.

JOY AFTER DIVORCE

Let's be honest. When we hold our marriages up to the straight edge of God's design for them, they are bent. Crooked. There are no exceptions. Even at their best, marriages that seek the glory of God fall far short of that lofty calling. There are not enough tears in the world for marriages that come to an end. No one enters marriage genuinely with its demise in view, but it happens, even for those who are followers of Christ. The glory of God is eclipsed by human failure. The possibilities of grace don't become realities. Instead there is disappointment, sorrow, frustration, anger, and pain. Vows are broken. Commitments are not honored. Or maybe the bond of love is simply too weak, and breaks beneath a burden of stress and the weight of the world. What began in faith, hope, and love ends in a painful parting of ways. I know some of these men and women. They are family and friends. We share life together in the same fellowship of faith. I grieve for them and confess that I am not one whit better.

If you are on the other side of divorce, how are these chapters relevant for you? You probably don't need to hear that God hates divorce,[15] but you may need to hear that he loves divorced people. There is only one unforgivable sin according to Jesus,[16] and it isn't divorce. Grace and mercy are offered to you. Will you accept them? Will you let them shape your life from this day on? God takes us where we are and seeks to move us forward. We can't change our past, but the power of the past can be broken in ways that will change our future.[17] I don't know how God will write the rest of your story, but I know that you can trust him with the tale. In his goodness he desires what is best for you, in his wisdom he knows how to bring it about, and in his unlimited power he is able to do it.[18]

If you are on the other side of divorce and you have children from your former marriage, there are still important roles for you to play in their lives.

Your children need your love: your nurturing and mentoring love, your friendship, and most of all the love of Christ through you.

Maybe you have remarried. Whether your divorce involved the unfaithfulness or abandonment of a spouse, or the embers of your love grew cold, I leave the moral factors in your divorce and remarriage in God's hands and your heart before him.[19] However you have come into your current marriage, I believe this to be true: God's plan for your life from this point on includes the marriage you are in. You should pursue everything we have talked about in this chapter and the two that precede it with great passion. If you have children from your earlier marriage, you still have a debt of love to them. It may have twists, turns, and complications that wouldn't otherwise have been factors in your life or theirs, but you must embrace them. If you are now in a blended family with stepchildren or children from this union, you have opportunities and responsibilities of love for your spouse and the children that are members of your household. Give yourself to these loves, and the joys of our gracious and merciful God can still be yours!

JOYFULLY SINGLE!

If you are single, what does our exploration of marriage and family have to do with you? If marriage is your hope and desire, my counsel to you is to pray daily for the man or woman that God may bring to you. What you don't know yet is fully disclosed to him. He knows that man, that woman, even if you don't. Pray and wait. Wait for the Lord. Wait for his timing. Let this ancient prayer be yours:

> But I trust in you, O LORD;
>   I say, "You are my God."
> My times are in your hand. (Psalm 31:14-15)

Pray that God will prepare this man or this woman for the four loves of marriage and family that we will explore in the next two chapters. As you seek the Lord and his good plan for your life, make these loves a focus of your prayer. Spend time with couples (young and old) in which you see these loves displayed. Learn from them.

If you are single, please wait for sex until you are married! Don't open that present until it is God's gift to you in marriage. Honor the marriage bed,[20] and God will honor you. It is worth the wait. I understand that our culture mocks chastity, but the Author of Life does not. He esteems it highly. Your commitment to him will be blessed in ways that are unknown to your peers. Your last laugh will be the best laugh, because it will be the laughter of joy. If, like many, you have fallen in this area of your life, it is as true for you today as it was when Jesus first spoke the words: Repentance is the doorway through which you must walk.[21] On the other side you will find grace, mercy, and the restored joys of salvation.[22]

Steward your singleness well. If you pursue joy, you will flourish in life as a single person, and bring your best to a marriage relationship. Cultivate your joy in God, his world, and his Word. Let the joy of salvation fill your heart. Develop joy in your work, joy in your play, joy in your creativity, and joy in your service for the Kingdom of God.

This is ironic but true: The greater your obsession with finding a spouse, the less you will be prepared for a healthy marriage. The more you focus on God-given joys in life before marriage and family, the greater your joy will be if and when God grants these relationships. If marriage and family exist for the glory of God, the best thing you can do is develop a passion for his glory in this God-appointed time of your life. Marriage should not be your purpose; that must be reserved for glorifying God and enjoying him. Make that your aim, and if God grants your request to be a husband or a wife, and a mother or a father, you will have stewarded your singleness well and prepared yourself to steward marriage and family life for his glory.

What about those who are not simply single, but celibate? All who are celibate are single,[23] but not all who are single are committed to a lifetime of celibacy. It is a special gift and a calling. Jesus spoke of it this way:

> Not everyone can receive this saying, but only those to whom it is given. For there are eunuchs who have been so from birth, and there are eunuchs who have been made eunuchs by men, and there are eunuchs who have made themselves eunuchs for the sake of the kingdom of heaven. Let the one who is able to receive this receive it. (Matthew 19:10-12)

After encouraging the church of Corinth to consider the advantages of being single, Paul wrote: "Now as a concession, not a command, I say this. I wish that all were as I myself am. But each has his own gift from God, one of one kind and one of another."[24] Earlier in that discourse he spoke of married couples abstaining temporarily from sexual relations so that they could better devote themselves to prayer. People who have been gifted and called to be celibate make this commitment for a lifetime. Celibacy is giving up a good for a higher good. Marriage and family are good gifts from God, but the Kingdom of God is greater.[25]

If this gift and calling are yours, you have more time to devote to the Kingdom. You have opportunities for joy that your married friends may well miss. God offers you joys that will be yours alone.

QUESTIONS FOR THOUGHT AND DISCUSSION

1. How does the notion of vocation help you understand marriage and family?

2. How does holiness fit into your understanding of marriage and family? What difference would it make for you to see these relationships set apart for and consecrated to God and his purposes for the world?

3. Read the following quote about Martin Luther. "[His] faith was simple enough to trust that after a conscientious day's labor, a Christian father could come home and eat his sausage, drink his beer, play his flute, sing with his children, and make love to his wife — all to the glory of God!" How is this different from what you've heard about marriage and the glory of God?

4. If you have been divorced, or know someone who has been, what prospects for joy do you see? How can you pursue this for yourself or encourage others who are on the other side of divorce?

5. If you are single, or know someone who is, how will you pursue joy in this time of your life? How can you help others pursue joy and singleness?

CHAPTER 4

LOVE'S DELIGHTS, PART 1

S torge, philia, eros, and *agape.* Ancient Greeks used these words to describe love. In English we would recognize them as affection, friendship, being in love, and charity.[1] When they are ours, these loves constitute a full, robust life. Together they hallow relationships and honor the God of love.[2]

These loves are essential to our joy. Josef Pieper wrote, "All love has joy as its natural fruit."[3] Joy is the beatitude of love. It is love's delight.[4] It is the pleasure of loving and being loved. In marriage and family these nuanced loves and their matching joys create a collage of pleasure that can't be found anywhere else. Only in these relationships can we experience all four loves and their delights without walking out our front door!

STORGE

C.S. Lewis saw *storge* as the humblest of the four loves that we will explore.[5] Its foundation is not shared interests (*philia*), or shared attraction (*eros*), but shared life. It is the bond that makes the familiarities of living together possible. It is the relational warmth that emanates from embers of shared time and space, and the rhythms and routines of life. It is the affection of mothers and fathers for their children, children for their parents, and sisters and brothers for each other. It is the cord that binds family and clan together.

Storge delights in a first word, a first tooth, and a first step. It walks a child to first grade, cheers a first homerun, and records a first recital. *Storge* celebrates birthdays, weddings, anniversaries, and family vacations. It prays in a hospital waiting room, holds vigil when death is near, puts flowers on a grave, and enshrines family memories in stories passed from one generation to another.

While *philia*, *eros*, and *agape* can exist without *storge*, it is unlikely that they will develop fully without it.[6] As Lewis put it, "A plant must have roots below as well as sunlight above."[7] To change and mix metaphors, *storge* is an anchor and a sail. It provides security and creates opportunity. It crafts a stable setting in which children grow and develop in healthy ways (which is why the plight of orphans is dire, and why children in broken and incomplete homes can be disadvantaged in life).

In a Christian vision of life, *storge* begins with the affirmation that marriage and family relationships are gifts from God and find their meaning in relation to him:[8]

> Therefore a man shall leave his father and his mother and hold fast to his wife, and the two shall become one flesh. . . . What therefore God has joined together, let not man separate (Matthew 19:5-6)

> He who finds a wife finds a good thing, and obtains favor from the LORD. (Proverbs 18:22)

> Behold, children are a heritage from the LORD,
>   the fruit of the womb a reward.
> Like arrows in the hand of warrior
>   are the children of one's youth.

Blessed is the man who fills his quiver with them! (Psalm 127:4-5)

[The LORD] gives the barren woman a home,
    making her the joyous mother of children. (Psalm 113:9)

Fathers, do not provoke your children to anger, but bring them up in the discipline and instruction of the Lord. (Ephesians 6:4)

Children, obey your parents in the Lord, for this is right. 'Honor your father and mother' (this is the first commandment with a promise), 'that it may go well with you and that you may live long in the land.' (Ephesians 6:1-3)

Lewis described *storge* in unflattering terms:

> It is indeed the least discriminating of loves. There are women for whom we can predict few wooers and men who are likely to have few friends. They have nothing to offer. But almost anyone can become an object of Affection; the ugly, the stupid, even the exasperating. There need be no apparent fitness between those whom it unites. I have seen it felt for an imbecile not only by his parents but by his brothers. It ignores the barriers of age, sex, class and education. It can exist between a clever young man from the university and an old nurse, though their minds inhabit different worlds.[9]

There is another way of looking at this. *Storge* is an everyday love. It is love wearing an apron, or work boots and gloves. It loves with or without merit. It loves even the unlovely. It is a strong, durable love. A faithful, steady, and unwavering love. *Storge* is an echo of God's parental love for us.[10] Like the father in Jesus' parable of the prodigal son,[11] God loves us even when we break his heart:

Children have I reared and brought up, but they have
    rebelled against me. (Isaiah 1:2)

When Israel was a child, I loved him,
    and out of Egypt I called my son.
The more they were called,
    the more they went away. . .
I led them with cords of kindness,
with the bands of love . . .
My people are bent on turn away from me. . .
How can I give you up, O Ephraim?
    How can I hand you over, O Israel? . . .
My heart recoils within me;
    My compassion grows warm and tender. (Hosea 11:1-8)

Like the fiercely devoted love of a mother, God's love for us never weakens, never ceases:

Can a woman forget her nursing child,
    that she should have no compassion on the son of her womb?
Even these may forget,
    yet I will not forget you. (Isaiah 49:15)

Storge is the love of parents for children, even in their waywardness. It is the love of children for parents, even with their shortcomings.[12] Luther wrote:

It must therefore be impressed on young people that they revere their parents as God's representatives, and to remember that, however lowly, poor, feeble, and eccentric they may be, they are still their mother and father, given by God. They are not to be deprived of their honor because of their ways or failings.[13]

Storge loves simply because families are God's creation and this affection is his design for them. It is fuel to a furnace, wind to a sail, water to a mill.

If it is true to God's design, *storge* is a nurturing and mentoring love. When it was written of Jesus in his boyhood that he "increased in wisdom and in stature, and in favor with God and man,"[14] it is a tribute to this love. God designed the process, and chose and prepared the family in which Jesus would be shaped by years of affectionate home life.

Storge is a stewarding love, shaped by a charge from God. Luther wrote:

> The greatest good in married life, that which makes all suffering and labor worthwhile, is that God grants offspring and commands that they be brought up to worship and serve him. In all the world this is the noblest and most precious work.[15]

> If our dear God and Father in heaven grants you children, nurture and care for them, raise them up in the discipline, fear, and admonition of the Lord. Then you will be doing right and performing better and nobler good works than all the monks and nuns; then you will be living in God's vocation and ordinance.[16]

Family affection is the current that carries wisdom from one generation to another:

> Hear, O Israel: The LORD our God, the LORD is one. You shall love the LORD your God will all your heart and with all your soul and with all your might. And these words that I command you today shall be on your heart. You shall teach them diligently to your children, and shall talk of them when you sit in your house, and when you walk by the way, and when you lie down and when you rise. (Deuteronomy 6:4-7)

LOVE'S DELIGHTS

> Hear, my son, your father's instruction,
>   and forsake not your mother's teaching. (Proverbs 1:8)

Storge equips children to flourish in life before God. It prepares girls to become godlywise women, and, if God wills, wives and mothers. It prepares boys to become godlywise men, and, if God wills, husbands and fathers. *Storge* is fulfilled in the priestly role of parents praying for their children, bringing them daily before the throne of grace, asking God to guide and direct, to provide and protect, and then seeking to be an answer to those prayers.

A family shaped by this love becomes a classroom of character. In this little community of intimate relationships, where life in its many facets is played out every day, children learn virtue from their parents. They learn Christ-likeness. Mothers and fathers model Christ, and children benefit from their example. Parents tell children stories of virtue and live out their own. Children are praised for their progress, encouraged for their efforts, held accountable for their words and deeds, and forgiven when they fail. Day after day, week after week, month after month, year after year, hearts are formed by the constancy of this love.[17]

Storge is a multi-generational love, from the first cry of a baby to the seasoned wisdom of a family's seniors, from kinder care to hospice care. (Ours is the loss when grandparents value retirement in a warmer climate more than they do sharing life with their children and grandchildren. Ours is the loss when advancement in a career, with its many moves, is more important than letting our children grow up with the experience of elder love.[18]   Ours is the loss when aunts, uncles, and cousins are only seen on Christmas cards.)   There is a wealth in family love that truly enriches. Beautiful tapestries of life are woven from family experiences that span generations. The joys that accompany this love cannot be found anywhere else.

PHILIA

Philia, or friendship, is a congenial love. It is based upon common beliefs, values, interests, and concerns, and the mutual enjoyment of people who share these things. Lewis wrote, "Without Eros none of us would have been begotten and without Affection none of us would have been reared; but we can live and breed without Friendship."[19] True, but we don't live well without it. You can find *philia* among neighborhood children, schoolmates, colleagues, and professional peers. You can discover it in churches, social organizations, book clubs, athletic teams, choirs, and bands, but it is formative and foundational in our lives when we experience it in marriage and family.

In family life *philia* and *storge* often overlap, or flow together. If my wife teaches our children culinary skills (because they would learn little from me), it is an expression of *storge*. If they come to enjoy the kitchen as she does, and they delight in preparing food together, it is *philia* enriching *storge*. If I teach our children the lore of hiking in the Rockies, this is *storge* in a mentoring role. If they come to love the mountains as I do, and we enjoy exploring them together, it is *philia* adding its touch to *storge*. Parents and children become friends. Their affection is strengthened by this love and enhanced by its joys. Brothers and sisters who know this love become friends for life.

What about *philia* between a man and a woman? It is wondrous, with dangers lurking nearby! Lewis wrote:

> When the two people who thus discover that they are on the same
> secret road are of different sexes, the friendship that arises between

them will very easily pass – may pass in the first half-hour – into erotic love. Indeed, unless they are physically repulsive to each other or unless one or both already loves elsewhere, it is almost certain to do so sooner or later.[20]

This is why it is dangerous to a marriage if a husband develops friendships with women other than his wife, or a wife with men other than her husband.[21] The power of our sexuality and the weakness of our fallen nature make us vulnerable. The same hazards exist for unmarried men and women when they "just want to be friends," but find that friendly affection pulled into sexual attraction whether it is their intent or not.

What if the friendship of a man and woman is fulfilled in marriage? It is cause for great celebration! It is expressed beautifully in the Song of Solomon: "This is my beloved and this is my friend."[22] *Philia* strengthens, deepens, and enriches a marriage relationship. When shared interests grow beyond children and the demands of nurture and provision, new pleasures and joys follow.[23] Shared worship, friendships, recreation, leisure, music, the arts, and social concern and action enhance married life. Couples who cultivate *philia* in their marriage discover joys in life that no other friends can know.

When *philia* is redeemed and shared, the common interests and concerns of friends center around joy in God, his world, his word, and his will.[24] Friendship at its highest and best includes friendship with Jesus.[25] When he is the Nexus in a relationship between friends, their joy includes his joy in them and theirs in him.

When *philia* is redeemed in marriages and families, they move closer to Eden. They are not yet all that God wants them to be, but they venture "further in and higher up"[26] than they can with *storge* alone. Husbands and wives, parents and children, sisters and brothers, truly enjoy each other. They don't merely share space under the same roof, they flourish in life together.

When they are friends in Christ, some of the greatest joys that can be known become theirs.

QUESTIONS FOR THOUGHT AND DISCUSSION

1. How has *storge* played out in the family you grew up in? How was/is it expressed? Was/is it a strong or a weak force? How do you want to do things differently in your own marriage and family?

2. What kind of mentoring and nurturing love did you experience growing up? Do you think you were prepared for marriage and family life yourself? How so? How not? How do you want to do things differently?

3. How do you see television, movies, video games, and unsupervised internet use impacting *storge* in family life? What commitments will you make in light of your response to these questions?

4. If you are married, how would you evaluate *philia* between you and your spouse? If you are single, how did you see *philia* play out in your parents' relationship?

5. If you are a parent, how would you evaluate *philia* with your children, and *philia* among your children? If you aren't yet a parent, how would you evaluate *philia* in what you know of your parents' relationship, and your relationship with your siblings? What can you do to strengthen this love?

CHAPTER 5

LOVE'S DELIGHTS, PART 2

EROS

*E*ros is what we mean when we talk about being in love.[1] It includes our sexuality, but it is more than this. It is possible to be familiar with the pleasures of sex and to be a foreigner to *eros*. Arranged marriages often include procreation and its pleasures without the presence of this love. The love of a husband and a wife, once robust with *eros*, can lapse into bedtime routines between emotional strangers. In our day, sex without *eros* has become epidemic among the unmarried. (Yes, I intended to say that. Keep reading and you will see why.) Unrestrained hedonism and mutual consent justify anything that can be imagined.

Popular opinion notwithstanding, *eros* and lust are not the same thing. Lust is fallen *eros*. It is a God-given desire that has been corrupted by our sin.[2] *Eros* is a flame lit by candles of desire and delight, attraction and admiration, enjoyment and esteem. Lust is a cold, calculating pursuit of pleasure. *Eros* is drawn to the beloved, desires the beloved, and is enraptured by the beloved. Lust seeks gratification. Period. C.S. Lewis wrote:

Sexual desire, without Eros, wants it, the thing in itself; Eros wants the Beloved. The thing is a sensory pleasure; that is, an event occurring within one's own body. We use a most unfortunate idiom when we say, of a lustful man prowling the streets, that he "wants a woman." Strictly speaking, a woman is just what he does not want. He wants a pleasure for which a woman happens to be the necessary piece of apparatus.[3]

Our confusion extends to marriage.[4] Husbands and wives can mistake lust for *eros*. If each uses the other for personal satisfaction, it is lust, not *eros*. If each is a taker and not a giver, it is lust, not *eros*. Couples who make this mistake believe that God approves because they once shared a wedding ceremony and now share life under the same roof. This way of thinking and acting degrades the gift of sex, demeans what God has made us to be as sexual beings, and despoils the sacred covenant of marriage.

Lust can be mistaken for *eros*. The opposite error occurs when *eros* is mistaken for lust. This happens when sex is framed by a dualistic understanding of the world in which the spiritual realm is good, and the physical realm – as such – is evil. In this vision of life, sex is castigated as a "carnal" pleasure. At best it is a necessary evil in the service of procreation; at worst it turns our hearts away from God and perverts true love. You can find this view among ancient Christian theologians who were influenced by Plato and his followers.[5] Here are a few examples of this error:

Our general argument concerning marriage, food, and other matters, may proceed to show that we should do nothing from desire. Our will is to be directed only towards that which is necessary. For we are children not of desire but of will. A man who marries for the sake of begetting children must practice continence so that it is not desire he feels for his wife, whom he ought to love, and that he may beget children with a chaste and controlled will.[6] *Clement of Alexandria (c. 150–215)*

"He who too ardently loves his own wife is an adulterer." It is disgraceful to love another man's wife at all, or one's own too much.

A wise man ought to love his wife with judgment, not with passion.[7] *Jerome (c. 347 – 420)*

In a good marriage, even with older people, although the passion of youth between man and woman has waned, the relationship of love between husband and wife continues strong, and the better persons they are, the earlier they begin by mutual consent to abstain from carnal union.[8] *Augustine (354 – 430)*

The commandment 'go forth and multiply' does not necessarily mean through conjugal union. For God could increase the human race by another means, if people had preserved the commandment inviolable to the end.[9] *John of Damascus (c. 645 -749).*

There are many in our day who can't connect the dots between God and sex, or if they do, the marks form a frown. God must surely avert his eyes from husbands and wives in bed! But what if there is a smile on the face of God as he delights in married couples enjoying the pleasures he designed and has given to them? If lust and *eros* are not the same, surely this is possible! John Calvin wrote, "Satan dazzles us . . . to imagine that we are polluted by intercourse. . . . [But] when the marital bed is dedicated to the name of the Lord, that is, when parties are joined together in his name, and live honorably, it is something of a holy estate."[10]   In a wedding sermon, Martin Luther wrote:

God's word is actually inscribed on one's spouse. When a man looks at his wife as if she were the only woman on earth, and when a woman looks at her husband if he were the only man on earth; yes, if no king or queen, not even the sun itself sparkles any more brightly and lights up your eyes more than your own husband or wife [a wonderful description of *eros*], then right there you are face to face with God speaking. God promises to you your wife or husband, actually gives your spouse to you saying, 'The man shall be yours. I am pleased beyond measure! Creatures earthly and heavenly are jumping for joy.'[11]

Eros includes our sexuality, but it is not first about sex. *Eros* is captivated and enchanted by the beloved. It longs for the beloved and delights in the beloved.[12] In God's design for marriage, sex follows powerfully and inevitably from this love. *Eros* reaches its full stature when it is the pleasure of loving and being loved, when we love to love,[13] when we give from our joy for the sake of our beloved's joy, when pleasure is mutual and delight is shared.

Play is a good gift from our good God. When *eros* is redeemed, sex (always and only in the sacred covenant of marriage) is love in a playful mode, engaged in a game in which each player seeks to out-give the other. Generosity is the measure of the game; pleasure-given-and-received is its prize. (In actual experience the giving and receiving are so thoroughly interlaced that it becomes impossible to distinguish them.)[14]

Eros-redeemed celebrates God's delight in our delight. It is a pleasure known to grateful hearts. In this way *eros* can become an expression of worship as much as any of his gifts that we offer back to him in thanksgiving and praise:

Now the Spirit expressly says that in later times some will depart from the faith . . . who forbid marriage and require abstinence from foods that God has created to be received with thanksgiving by those who believe and know the truth. For everything created by God is good, and nothing is to be rejected if it is received with thanksgiving, or it is made holy by the word of God and prayer. (1 Timothy 4:1-5)

This puts us in the best position to understand *The Song of Solomon* and its inclusion in the canon of Scripture. It isn't an allegory. It is a celebration of *eros*. It revels in the enjoyment of sexual love. It is sex as sacred play. Even if the Ancient Near Eastern imagery seems strange to us, we are invited to affirm the goodness of husbands and wives delighting in each other before God:

> Let him kiss me with the kisses of his mouth!
> For your love is better than wine. . . (1:2)

> As an apple tree among the trees of the forest,
>   so is my believed among the young men.
> With great delight I sat in his shadow,
>   and his fruit was sweet to my taste.
> He brought me to the banqueting house,
>   and his banner over me was love.
> Sustain me with raisins,
>   refresh me with apples,
>   for I am sick with love.
> His left hand is under my head,
>   and his right hand embraces me! (2:3-6)

> You have captivated my heart, my sister, my bride;
>   you have captivated my heart with one glance of your eyes,
>   with one jewel of your necklace.
> How beautiful is your love, my sister, my bride!
>   How much better is your love than wine,

and the fragrance of your oils than any spice! (4:9-10)

> How beautiful and pleasant you are,
>   O loved one, with all your delights!
> Your stature is like a palm tree,
>   and your breasts are like its clusters.
> I say I will climb the palm tree
>   and lay hold of its fruit.
> Oh may your breasts be like clusters of the vine,
>   and the scent of your breath like apples,
> and your mouth like the best wine. (7:7-9)

Eros is good, because it is the gift of a good God. It is included in our joy, because it is the gift of a joyful God.

When *eros* is redeemed, sexual love is a reaffirmation of marital vows. Each time anew, sexual union embraces vows given and received in the presence of God on a couple's wedding day. It is a recommitment to their sacred covenant. Sexual love strengthens the bonds of marriage through giving and receiving, mutual fulfillment of God-given desires, and a shared pleasure in God and his good gifts.

When *eros* joins the voices of *storge* and *philia* in marriage, the trio echoes the ancient harmony of Eden. The coupling of a husband and wife before God becomes healthy, robust, and joyful, because it moves closer to God's design at the dawn of our creation.

AGAPE

We come at last to *agape*, the highest of the four loves.[15] In God's design, *storge*, *philia*, and *eros* prepare our hearts for this love. They are *agape's* early lessons:

From the first coupling of the parents in desire for each other and for fruit, through the carrying of the first child by the mother and the husband's consideration for his pregnant wife, on through the suckling and feeding, to the training of the children ("Say 'thank you,'" or "Pick up your paper dolls," or "Stand up when your mother comes into the room,") and the ordinary muddle of things done together, it is all the school of Charity. For is not Charity the name given to that final, perfect, gloriously free and blissful state where all the lessons have been so mastered that the rules ("Pick up your paper dolls," or "Thou shalt not steal") have withered, and all of us have won through to the capacity to experience as joy, the thing that was hinted at in all our early lessons; namely, that My Life For Yours is the principle at the bottom of everything, to embrace which is to live and to refuse which is to die?[16]

The true glory of *storge*, *philia*, and *eros* emerges when they bow before the highest love. They become most fully themselves and most fully offer their unique contributions to life when they do. As Lewis put it, "In this yoke lies their true freedom; they 'are taller when they bow.'"[17]

Agape is the most Godlike of the loves, because it is pure Gift-love. When we say that God is love,[18] and that he is the Giver of every good and perfect gift,[19] we are saying the same thing in different ways. In creation we see God's love as he "gives life and breath to all."[20] In redemption, he loves the world and gives his only Son.[21] The Son gives his life as a ransom for a world held hostage in sin.[22] The Spirit is given to us,[23] and he bestows the boon of his presence.[24] The Gifting-God loves to give. This is *agape*.

Agape is unconditional, but not invincible. It is the most powerful of the loves because of what it can accomplish; it is often the most tragic of the loves, because its aspirations are so high and it can be scorned. If we allow *agape* to shape our loves, we must accept the risk that comes with it:

There is no safe investment. To love at all is to be vulnerable. Love anything, and your heart will certainly be wrung and possibly be broken. If you want to make sure of keeping it intact, you must give your heart to no one, not even to an animal. Wrap it carefully round with hobbies and little luxuries; avoid all entanglements; lock it up safe in the casket or coffin of your selfishness. But in that casket, safe, dark, motionless, airless – it will change. It will not be broken; it will become unbreakable, impenetrable, irredeemable. The alternative to the risk of tragedy, is damnation. The only place outside Heaven where you can be perfectly safe from all the dangers and perturbations of love is Hell.[25]

By his sovereign permission, even God's love can be unrequited.[26] He allows his love to be refused.[27] When it is, his heart is broken. There is love-rejected in the poignant words of Jesus as he stands in *loco Dei*,[28] addressing the Holy City: "O Jerusalem, Jerusalem, the city that kills the prophets and stones those who are sent to it! How often would I have gathered your children together as a hen gathers her brood under her wings, and you were not willing!" [29]

Even if it can be spurned, *agape* is the most potent of the loves. It is *agape*, and only *agape*, that can save our world. It is a love expressed most powerfully in the cross of Christ:[30] "For while we were still weak, at the right time Christ died for the ungodly. For one will scarcely die for a righteous person—though perhaps for a good person one would dare even to die – but God shows his love for us in that while we were still sinners, Christ died for us."[31] There is no greater love than this. Christ did not die for the godly (there are none), or for those with merit (a class without members), but for those who deserve only judgment (all of us). The Righteous One gave his life for an unrighteous world.[32] This is the greatest love our world can know. The river of redemption has its headwaters here.

Agape can transform our lives because it transforms our loves and renovates their domains in life. *Agape* changes *storge's* ordinary love between family members into something extraordinary. It infuses families with a power to love when loving would not be their normal response. *Agape* brings with it the other fruit of the Spirit: joy, peace, patience, kindness, goodness, faithfulness, gentleness, and self-control,[33] and these virtues of love shape every facet of marriage and family life.

Agape can transform *philia*: "Greater love has no one than this: than to lay down one's life for one's friends."[34] When this happens, friends not only enjoy common interests and enjoy each other, they share a common commitment: Each would give his or her life for the other. Imagine a family in which a woman knows that her husband would gladly die for her, a man knows that his wife would willingly give her life for him, and children know that their parents would surrender their lives for them without hesitation or hint of regret. There is no stronger bond of friendship. There are no stronger families than those who share this love.

Agape can transform *eros*. The paradox of hedonism is that the more you seek pleasure, the more it goes bad on you. But this is only true if the pleasure you are seeking is your own! There is a very different paradox in play when *agape* transforms *eros*: The more you seek the pleasure of your beloved, the greater your pleasure, and the greater your joy. "I am my beloved's, and my beloved is mine."[35] This is *eros*. It is a good gift. *Eros* needs the beloved, can't bear to live without him, cannot endure without her. *Agape* raises *eros* to a higher level when it says, "I am my beloved's, my beloved is mine, and we are God's." He becomes the apex of their relationship, the highest point that their love together can reach.

Inscribed in the Bible that was given to me by my wife more than twenty-five years ago are these words:

Dearest Rick,

For my husband who points me to Christ each day by the life he lives. My love through His,

Sue

"My love through His." *Agape* is the most Godlike of the loves, but there is more to it than this. God "communicates to men a share of His own Gift-love."[36] He loves through us. We love through his love. *Agape* integrates our loves and transposes them into something higher and better. Transformed by *agape*, *storge*, *philia* and *eros* are ennobled and enriched by God's touch. They are empowered by his love coursing through them.

Joy is love's delight.[37] When joy is the beatitude of the four loves in the richly colored and textured relationships of marriage and family, there is no other beauty like it in our world. No other fragrance has its allure. The joys of *storge*, *philia*, *eros*, and *agape*, experienced in day-to-day life in marriages and families, bring us as close to Eden as we will get in this chapter of the human story.

The spiritual significance of marriage and family can be easily missed because we are so close to these relationships, so caught up in them. There is great power in these words:

> I would like to suggest that at least one place (among others) which may be hallowed anew as the place where all the celebration of all the mysteries may occur, and where all of life may be offered up in oblation to the Most High, is the family household. Within these four walls, under this roof, the lamps are lighted. The offering is here, the vigil is here, the feast is here, the faithful are here. All the eating and drinking, and the working and playing, and the discipline and serving and loving that go on here – they are all holy.

For these common routines of ordinary life are not only necessities and functions: they are also messengers to us from the hallows. Nay, more than messengers, they are those hallows, set hourly before us in visible, touchable, light-of-day forms.[38]

"O God, bring these truths into our marriages and our families! Bring these loves! Make them realities in our lives! What we receive from you we offer back to you in worship. These relationships, these loves, this joy, we offer to the world for its greater good and your greater glory. Amen."

QUESTIONS FOR THOUGHT AND DISCUSSION

1. After reading this chapter, how is lust different from *eros*, and how does that challenge views you have held?

2. Read the following quote.

   > There are many in our day who cannot connect the dots between God and sex, or if they do, the marks form a scowl or at least a frown. God must surely avert his eyes from husbands and wives in bed! But what if the dots form a smile on the face of God as he delights in married couples enjoying the pleasures that he himself designed and has given to them?

   How does viewing *eros* as a good gift from our good God challenge your understanding of this love?

3. In what ways can *agape* redeem *storge*, and what would that look like in your life?

4. In what ways can *agape* redeem *philia*, and what would that look like in your life?

5. In what ways can *agape* redeem *eros*? What implications does this have for you? How could this change our culture?

ABOUT THE AUTHOR

In 1983 Rick and Sue Howe moved to Boulder, Colorado, where they raised three children – Amberle, Lorien, and Jamison – and have devoted more than thirty years to campus ministry at the University of Colorado. In addition to writing and speaking, Rick now leads University Ministries, whose mission is to "inspire and nurture a thoughtful pursuit of Christ, one student, one professor, one university at a time." To learn more about Rick, visit his website at www.rickhowe.org. You can also follow him on Facebook at *Rick Howe on Joy* and on Twitter @rickhoweonjoy. To learn more about University Ministries, see www.university-ministries.org.

ENDNOTES

PREFACE

[1]   Proverbs 17:22

[2]   Dallas Willard, *Renovation of the Heart: Putting on the Character of Christ* (Colorado Springs, CO: NavPress, 2002), p. 133.

[3]   Peter Kreeft, *Heaven: The Heart's Deepest Longing* (San Francisco: Ignatius Press, Expanded Edition, 1980), p. 129.

CHAPTER 1: EDEN'S JOY

¹ While I acknowledge that contemporary genetic evidence and other postulates of evolutionary theory represent a challenge that should engage Christians in serious thinking and dialogue, I did not come to my belief (nor will I abandon my belief) in a historical Adam and Eve, an original Edenic environment in which they lived, and a state of innocence from which they fell, on the basis of scientific inquiry.

The Scriptures are the "norming norm" for my faith. I make no apologies for this. Indeed, it is a great joy to me! Having said this, the ancient texts of Scripture must be read first – as much as possible – with their original audience in mind. We should resist the temptation of importing our interests and concerns into the way we understand them, and forcing them to take up arms in our conflicts.

I recognize that the Hebrew word *adam* was used for humanity as a whole as well as for an individual in the Genesis story (Adam = Mankind). I can also see how Israel, in its exile from the promised land, would have seen itself in Adam and his expulsion from the Garden (Adam = Israel). Neither of these observations, however, negates the possibility that Adam was also viewed as a historical figure. (Compare Jacob = Israel.) Neither seems to factor into the canonical context of Jesus' teaching on marriage and divorce in Matthew 19, and Paul's exposition of redemptive history in Romans 5 – both of which posit a historical Adam.

While Jesus does not refer to an original pair by name, his affirmation of the Creator's original intention for marriage clearly has the Edenic couple in mind. ("He who created them from the beginning made them male and female, and said, 'Therefore a man shall leave his father and his mother and hold fast to his wife, and the two shall become one flesh.'" On the matter of divorce, he affirms an original state of innocence from which humanity has lapsed ("From the beginning it was not so.")

In Romans 5, Israel as a nation is not in view. The "one man" (Adam) is distinguished from all who followed from him ("all men"). In this passage we do see the Jewish penchant for seeing deeper meanings in their stories. Adam is not an archetype for humanity or for Israel, however, but a "type" of Christ. This is the frame of reference in which we should pursue our interpretation. The parallels are between two men (Adam and Christ), sin entering the world through one and grace through the other, an act of disobedience and an act of righteousness, judgment and justification, death and eternal life. Any other frame of reference is alien to the context. In a grand metanarrative, Paul lays out the themes of Creation, Fall, and Redemption: one man in the beginning from whom humanity sprang and through whose "act of disobedience" sin entered the world, a historical period ("from Adam to Moses"), and God's saving action through the one man, Jesus Christ ("the one who was to come").

I affirm that there is great value in the scientific enterprise, and believe that if we love God with our minds (in fulfillment of the greatest commandment) we will boldly declare that all truth is his – wherever it is found – and we will pursue it to the best of our abilities under God. I also affirm the priority and supremacy of the Scriptures for our faith, and what seems to me to be the clear teaching of Jesus and Paul. This leads me to a confident belief that whatever we may say about the age of the universe and the development of life on our planet, there was an original couple who bore the image of God without flaw, were placed in an Edenic setting of innocence, fell from that state through a primal act of disobedience, and brought sin into the world as well as all future generations of humans who fallibly bear the image of God.

For a contemporary discussion, see Matthew Barrett and Ardel B. Caneday, eds. *Four Views on the Historical Adam* (Grand Rapids: Zondervan, 2013).

[2] Karl Barth discusses the relationship between the triunity and the joy of God:

> As the triunity – and by this we mean in the strictest and most proper sense, God Himself – is the basis of the power and dignity of the divine being, and therefore, also of His self-declaration, His glory, so this triune being and life (in the strict and proper sense, God Himself) is the basis of what makes this power and dignity enlightening, persuasive and convincing. For this is the particular function of this form. *It is radiant, and what it radiates is joy. It attracts and therefore it conquers. It is, therefore, beautiful. But it is this, as we must affirm, because it reflects the triune being of God.* It does not do this materially, so that a triad is to be found in it. It does it formally, which is the only question that can now concern us. It

does this to the extent that in it there is repeated and revealed the unity and distinction of the divine being particular to it as the being of the triune God. To this extent the triunity of God is the secret of His beauty. If we deny this, we at once have a God without radiance and without joy (and without humour!); a God without beauty (emphasis added).

Karl Barth, *Church Dogmatics*, eds., Geoffrey W. Bromiley, T. F. Torrance (New York: Charles Scribner's Sons, 1957), Vol. II, p. 661. Emphasis added.

3   Genesis 1:10, 12, 18, 21, 25, 31

4   Genesis 2:18

5   Karl Barth gave emphasis to this in his understanding of the *imago Dei*:

> "He created them male and female." This is the interpretation immediately given to the sentence "God created man." As in this sense man is the first and only one to be created in genuine confrontation with God and as a genuine counterpart to his fellows, it is he first and alone who is created "in the image" and "after the likeness" of God.
>
> "And God created man in his image, in the image of God created he him; male and female he created them." . . . Could anything be more obvious than to conclude from this clear indication that the image and likeness of the being created by God signifies existence in confrontation, i.e., in this confrontation, in the juxtaposition and conjunction of man and man which is that of male and female, and then go on to ask against this background in what the original and prototype of the divine existence of the Creator consists? "These two, male and female, are to Him 'man' because they are one before Him. Both are created in this divine image, so that the enjoyment of the divine felicity – to the extent that a creature was made capable of receiving it – was communicated to man as a married couple, filled by God and in God with mutual divine love, from which we may understand and conclude the high dignity of marriage.

Karl Barth, Church *Dogmatics*, eds., G.W. Bromiley, T.F. Torrance (London, New York: T & T Clark International, 2004), Vol. 3.1, pp. 184, 195.

D.S. Bailey writes: "Man . . . is in the image of God in its Manward aspect primarily by virtue of his essential structure as a bi-personal male-female unity in which (relationally . . . not numerically) the coinherence of Father, Son and Holy Spirit is reflected in terms of finite existence." Quoted in Colin Gunton, "The Church on Earth: The Roots of Community," found at: http://theologicaleducationorg.files.wordpress.com/2012/03/ gunton.pdf.

6   Although marriage is an important way in which the image of God is played out in human life, it is not a necessary property of the image of God. If it were, the following would necessarily be the case:

> Humans do not bear the image of God outside of marriage (which means, among other things, that children do not).

> Either Jesus failed, or was secretly married as the Gnostics believed.

> Either Jesus was wrong in saying that there would be no marriage in the resurrection, or we will cease to be image-bearers in that state. (Matthew 22:30)

> Both Jesus and Paul were wrong in advocating singleness for the sake of the Kingdom. (Matthew 19:12 and 1 Corinthians 7:8)

There is a better way to understand marriage and the image of God:

> Marriage is not essential, but consequential, to being in the image of God. It is a secondary feature of the image. It adds rich features to our likeness to God.

> Gendered relations ("male and female he created them") are fundamental to the image of God regardless of marital status. We are fundamentally made to be beings-in-relation, and this reflects something of the transcendent relations of the persons of the Trinity.

Marriage serves the purposes of the imago Dei for God's glory and our joy.

7   In Hebrew, man and woman are *ish* and *ishshah*.

8   Analogy of being (*analogia entis*). It is not a matter of projecting human traits onto our understanding of God. The knowledge *of* God can only be knowledge *from* God. The analogy is both established and revealed by God.

9   Both the original creation account and Jesus' re-telling of the story to teach about marriage affirm the goodness of sexual intercourse between a man and a woman in a life-long covenant relationship, and do not envision any other relationship as an appropriate context for that intimate interaction.

10   A life-long covenant is as close as we come to the eternal bond of love in the Trinity. Divorce diminishes the image of God in the world.

11   Pope John Paul II wrote:

> Man became the 'image and likeness' of God not only through his own humanity, but also through the communion of persons which man and woman form right from the beginning. . . . Right 'from the beginning,' he is not only an image in which the solitude of a person who rules the world is reflected, but also, and essentially, an image of an inscrutable divine communion of persons."

Pope John Paul II, *The Theology of the Body: Human Love in the Divine Plan* (Boston: Pauline Books and Media, 1997), p. 46.

According to Stanley Grenz:

> The meaning of marriage arises out of the place of this institution within the purposes of the Creator. This meaning is enhanced by the biblical use of marriage as a metaphor of God and God's people. However, there remains yet a further dynamic, one which brings together the Old and New Testament uses of the male-female bond.

Both in itself and in its relationship to the church, marriage can be a fitting symbol or metaphor of the triune nature of God.

Stanley J. Grenz, *Sexual Ethics: A Biblical Perspective* (Dallas: Word Publishing, 1990), p. 51.

James Torrance has written, "God is love and has his true being in communion, in the mutual indwelling of Father, Son and Holy Spirit . . . This is the God who has created us male and female in his image to find our true humanity in . . . unity with him and one another." James B. Torrance, *Worship, Community and the Triune God of Grace* (Downers Grove: InterVarsity Press, 1996), p. 39.

[12] The Hebrew word translated help or helper, used of Eve in her relationship with Adam in Genesis 2:18, is *ezer*. I've never understood why some see connotations of inferiority in this title. It seems an odd way of thinking that the one who needs help is superior to the one who provides it. The same word is used of God himself in his relationship with his people. See, e.g., the following:

> Our soul waits for the LORD; he is our help and our shield. (Psalm 33:20).

> But I am poor and needy; hasten to me, O God!
> You are my help and my deliverer; O LORD, do not delay! (Psalm 70:5)

> O Israel, trust in the LORD! He is their help and their shield. (Psalm 115:9)
> My help comes from the LORD, who made heaven and earth. (Psalm 121:2)

[13] "The man called his wife's name Eve, because she was the mother of all living." (Genesis 3:20)

[14] The Hebrew word *Adam* was used both of humanity (mankind, or humankind) as a whole, and of the first man. In the opening chapter of Genesis, *Adam* is the former; in chapter two he is the latter.

[15] I take the verb "to husband," to mean "to steward resources." It comes from an old Norse word which referred to a "tiller of soil." I acknowledge that this meaning is not present in the Hebrew for Adam. It seems fitting, however, for two reasons: 1) In creation, Eve's "man" understood his role in the world to be a steward, including

the Garden; 2) In redemption, husbands are charged with stewarding their marriage with the goal of presenting their wives to Christ in the fullness of their feminine glory (Ephesians 5:25-27). I understand this to have a special focus on encouragement and empowerment. Husbands ought to encourage and empower their wives to become all that they can be in Christ.

Stewardship involves the management of something that belongs to someone else. Eve did not belong to Adam, but to God. This truth exposes the lie – wherever it is found – that a wife is the property of her husband. Husbanding and helping both focus on a supportive commitment that enables the beloved to become most fully what God intends him or her to be.

[16] "Then the LORD God said, 'It is not good that the man should be alone; I will make him a helper fit for him.'" (Genesis 2:18)

[17] "Now Adam knew Eve his wife, and she conceived and bore Cain, saying, 'I have gotten a man with the help of the LORD.'" (Genesis 4:1) Because this "knowing," which resulted in the conception and birth of Cain, took place after the expulsion from the Garden, some ancient commentators believed that sex was a result of the Fall. For instance, Augustine wrote, "For it was after they were expelled from it [Paradise] that they came together to beget children, and begot them." Saint Augustine, *The City of God*, trans. Marcus Dods (New York, NY: The Modern Library, 1950), p. 469.

Some believed that the first couple would have had children without sex if they hadn't fallen into sin. John of Damascus (c. 645-749) wrote, "The commandment 'go forth and multiply' does not necessarily mean through conjugal union. For God could increase the human race by another means, if people had preserved the commandment inviolable to the end." Quoted in Vladimir Moss, *Eros in Orthodox Thought*, found at: http://www.romanitas.ru/eng/EROS.htm.

The most that can be said from Genesis 4:1 is that intercourse resulting in pregnancy and childbirth happened after the Fall. Sexual union was clearly envisioned in chapter 1 in the blessing to be fruitful and multiply, and in chapter 2 in the Creator's design for them to be "one flesh" and the fact that they were "naked and unashamed."

If we were to draw any conclusions from Genesis 4:1, it would most naturally be that sex was initially a gift designed solely for the pleasure of Adam and Eve in the "honeymoon" phase of their relationship. When Eve did later conceive, it is as if something new and different had happened in her union with Adam – "with the help of the LORD." Were it not for sin, in time Adam and Eve would have had children in the Garden, and their children would have had children after them. It is not childbearing as such that was introduced in the Curse, but pain in childbearing (Genesis 3:16).

If you embrace the view that human gender and sexuality are part of bearing the image of God, and that sex is as much about the pleasures of an intimate relationship between a husband and wife as it is about procreation, sex before the Fall is exactly what you would expect to have happened.

[18]   Genesis 2:25

[19]   Singleness and celibacy come into play later in our human story. As Jesus was, we can be fully human and fulfilled in life without marriage. However, that was not God's design for the beginning of our race.

[20]   For the first couple, their bodies were not the boundaries of their intimacy. More profoundly, it was an entwining of hearts. A giving and receiving of their innermost life. The deep center of their intimacy was a shared worship and a shared joy. A common love for their Creator and mutual pleasure in him. Their love for each other was shaped by their love for him, and kindled by his love for them. Their joy in each other included an awareness of their Maker rejoicing over them, blessing their union, and pleased with their pleasure. Their intimacy was two-fold: husband and wife with each other, and with the God who made them and was present with them in all of life.

[21]   Genesis 1:28

[22]   When I give premarital counseling to a couple that does not want or intend to have children, it raises important questions of values that I am compelled to ask: Why would you not want children? Is it possible that what God calls a blessing you see as a burden, or even a curse? If so, that is a problem!

If children are a blessing from the Lord, then couples should at least have what Pope John Paul II called a "procreative attitude," even if they have good reasons for family planning. I agree that this attitude is healthy and important. It means that a husband and wife must "acquire and possess solid convictions about the true values of life and of the family." See Pope John Paul II, *Theology*, p. 399.

23 I understand why one might interpret these words as an imperative. It is grammatically possible. In Hebrew (like the English future tense) the imperfect tense can function to indicate future action or mandated action. Context must help determine which is the case. When the imperfect tense is used in the language of blessing, it is a forecast of the future enabled and assured by the favor and resources of the one giving the blessing.

24 The Unification Church believes that this, indeed, was Jesus' failure; which is why another Messiah had to come who would fulfill what they take to be a creation mandate.

25 Genesis 1:22

26 See, for example:

> And if you faithfully obey the voice of the LORD your God, being careful to do all his commandments that I command you today, the LORD your God will set you high above all the nations of the earth. And all these blessings shall come upon you and overtake you, if you obey the voice of the LORD your God. Blessed shall you be in the city, and blessed shall you be in the field. Blessed shall be the fruit of your womb and the fruit of your ground and the fruit of your cattle, the increase of your herds and the young of your flock. Blessed shall be your basket and your kneading bowl. Blessed shall you be when you come in, and blessed shall you be when you go out.

> The LORD will cause your enemies who rise against you to be defeated before you. They shall come out against you one way and flee before you seven ways. The LORD will command the blessing on you in your barns and in all that you undertake. And he will bless you in the land that the LORD your God is giving you. The LORD will establish you as a people

holy to himself, as he has sworn to you, if you keep the commandments of the LORD your God and walk in his ways. And all the peoples of the earth shall see that you are called by the name of the LORD, and they shall be afraid of you. And the LORD will make you abound in prosperity, in the fruit of your womb and in the fruit of your livestock and in the fruit of your ground, within the land that the LORD swore to your fathers to give you. The LORD will open to you his good treasury, the heavens, to give the rain to your land in its season and to bless all the work of your hands. And you shall lend to many nations, but you shall not borrow. (Deuteronomy 28:1-12)

27 As one scholar puts it: "In the Bible blessing means primarily the active outgoing of the divine goodwill or grace which results in prosperity and happiness amongst men." Alan Richardson, ed., *A Theological Word Book of the Bible* (New York: The Macmillan Co., 1958) p. 33.

28 "He who finds a wife finds a good thing and obtains favor from the LORD." (Proverbs 18:22)

29 We will see this theme in Song of Solomon for Chapter 12. It is also found in the book of Proverbs:

> Let your fountain be blessed,
>   and rejoice in the wife of your youth,
>   a lovely deer, a graceful doe.
> Let her breasts fill you at all times with delight;
>   be intoxicated always in her love. (Proverbs 5:18-19)
>
> Three things are too wonderful for me . . .
>   the way of an eagle in the sky . . .
>   the way of a ship on the high seas,
>   and the way of a man with a maiden. (Proverbs 30:18-19, RSV)

30 Luther commented:

> For this word which God speaks, 'Be fruitful and multiply,' is not a command. It is more than a command, namely, a divine ordinance

which it is not our prerogative to hinder or ignore. Rather, it is just as necessary as the fact that I am a man, and more necessary than sleeping and waking, eating and drinking, and emptying the bowels and bladder. It is a nature and disposition just as innate as the organs involved in it. Therefore, just as God does not command anyone to be a man or a woman but created them the way they have to be, so he does not command them to multiply but creates them so that they have to multiply.

"The Christian in Society" II, in *Luther's Works*, ed. Helmut T. Lehmann (Philadelphia: Muhlenberg Press, 1962), Vol. 45, p. 18.

[31]   Children are a blessing from God. They are meant for our joy:

> The LORD is high above all nations,
>   and his glory above the heavens!
> Who is like the LORD our God,
>   who is seated on high,
> Who looks far down
>   on the heavens and the earth?
> He raises the poor from the dust,
>   and lifts the needy from the ash heap
> to make them sit with princes
>   with the princes of his people.
> He gives the barren woman a home,
>   making her the joyous mother of children.
> Praise the LORD! (Psalm 113:4-9)

> Behold, children are a heritage from the LORD,
>   the fruit of the womb a reward . . .
> Blessed is the man who fills his quiver with them. (Psalm 127:3, 5)

> Your wife will be like a fruitful vine within your house;
>   your children will be like olive shoots around your table.
> Behold, thus shall the man be blessed who fears the LORD. (Psalm 128:3-4)

32   Some couples are unable to have children as the fruit of their union. On this side of the Garden and the Fall, adoption is a wonderful way of mirroring God's redeeming love or us in Christ!

33   Genesis 3:15, known as the proto-gospel:

> I will put enmity between you and the woman,
>> and between your offspring and her offspring;
> he shall bruise your head,
>> and you shall bruise his heel.

Galatians 4:4-5 views this maternal event from the other side: "But when the fullness of time had come, God sent forth his Son, born of woman, born under the law, to redeem those who were under the law, so that we might receive adoption as sons."

The final link in the generational chain involved a Virgin Birth, but this would not have been possible (and the genealogies of Jesus are given to emphasize this) without normal marriage and childbearing for thousands of years leading up to that redemptive event.

34   In his discussion of the "The Nuptial Meaning of the Body," Pope John Paul II, reflects the Catholic tradition when he speaks of "man's original happiness," and again in his exposition on "The Mystery of Man's Original Innocence." Pope John Paul II, *Theology*, pp. 61 and 67ff.

If I had to guess, Protestant theologians have been reluctant to go there because they want to distance themselves from the Catholic position on original sin and its view of the remnants of the imago Dei that have survived the Fall.

35   This is the joy which Madeleine L'Engle sees captured in the Sanskrit word, *ananda*: "that joy in existence, without which the universe will fall apart and collapse." Madeleine L'Engle, *A Swiftly Tilting Planet* (New York, NY: Dell Publishing, 1979), p. 40. This was not lost entirely in the Fall (Or I would not be here to write this, and you would not be here to read it!), but it was fractured and must be repaired.

CHAPTER 2: FAR AS THE CURSE IS FOUND

¹ "For they sow the wind, and they shall reap the whirlwind." (Hosea 8:7)

² The heinous moral reality behind "partial birth abortion."

³ Lyrics by the English hymn writer, Isaac Watts. It was written originally to celebrate the return of Christ at the end of the age, and not his nativity. What will be true in full then can be true now in part.

⁴ Restoring the joys of marriage can only happen as those who are married embrace the joys of salvation. I can offer no hope and no joy apart from that.

⁵ Not all politicians would do this, of course, but those of us who watch the news see such things all too often!

⁶ All who sincerely pray, "May your kingdom come, may your will be done on earth as it is in heaven" embrace an ideal that is impossible on human terms. We should not be surprised that this is true when we bring our marriage into that prayer.

⁷ "The disciples said to him, 'If such is the way of a man with his wife, it is better not to marry.'" (Matthew 19:10)

⁸ There were two schools of thought on the grounds for divorce. The stricter view was held by Rabbi Shammai, who taught that adultery alone was grounds for divorce. The more liberal view was held by Rabbi Hillel, who taught that a Jewish man could divorce his wife for any reason, from a burnt meal to the discovery of another woman whom he considered more beautiful. The latter was the dominant view in Jesus' day. See, e.g., William Barclay, *The Gospel of Matthew*, revised edition (Philadelphia: The Westminster Press, 1975), Vol. II, pp. 198-199.

⁹ "He said to them, 'Because of your hardness of heart Moses allowed you to divorce your wives, but from the beginning it was not so.'" (Matthew 19:8)

¹⁰ Matthew 19:26

11 The first step in reaching any goal is believing that it is possible. For the follower of Jesus this involves believing that something is possible because God himself is involved and invested in the outcome, and then prayerfully acting on that possibility. See the invitation of Jesus in Matthew 17:19-20, Mark 11:22-24, and Luke 17:5-7.

12 Stanley Grenz wrote:

> The concept of trinitarian community is closely related to the divine attribute of love. Throughout the Bible God is presented as the loving one. . . . This assertion suggests that the community that comprises the Godhead is likewise best characterized by reference to the concept of love. The doctrine of the Trinity – the affirmation of one God in three persons – allows this idea to be taken a step further. It indicates that the bonding that characterizes the divine life is similar to the dialectic of sameness and difference found in human sexuality.

Stanley J. Grenz, *Sexual Ethics: A Biblical Perspective* (Dallas, et al.: Word Publishers, 1990), p. 36.

13 I grant that marriage can be viewed as a civil union. Luther saw it that way. This is the realm of government. It is the framework of the contemporary debate about marriage, gender, and sexual orientation. Classically, government would have concerned itself with whether the social order and well-being of citizens is best served by a union between a man and a woman, and by children having both a mother and a father, or by same-gendered partnerships and parenting. In our day the focus has shifted to the pursuit of happiness, however one construes it, and rights to private and public benefits and services.

Whatever you think about these issues, the New Testament sees marriage not as a social contract before human courts, but a sacred covenant before God. There it is portrayed as a relationship between a man and a woman, with Christ as its nexus, summit, and center, and children, if they are granted, as its boon.

It is tragic to see Christians arguing so stridently about civil unions when our own sacred covenants are failing. Nero fiddles while Rome burns! The real power for transforming our culture is not government legislation and the judicial recognition of social contracts (however they are constituted, and however contemporary debates turn out), but the beauty, fragrance, and health of the sacred covenant of marriage on as large a scale as possible.

Even if we have deep moral disagreements over issues of gender identity and sexual orientation, the love we are commanded to show our neighbor includes all without distinction. The command cuts in all directions, and allows no exceptions.

For those who fret about non-traditional civil unions, according to a 2013 national survey reported by the Center for Disease Control and Prevention, only 1.6% of American adults self-identify as gay or lesbian, and only 0.7% consider themselves bi-sexual. Only a fraction of these enter into civil unions. A sense of proportion would be prudent. See: http://www.washingtonpost.com/national/health-science/health-survey-gives-government-its-first-large-scale-data-on-gay-bisexual-population/2014/07/14/2db9f4b0-092f-11e4-bbf1-cc51275e7f8f_story.html.

[14] "Then the man said, 'This at last is bone of my bones and flesh of my flesh; she shall be called Woman, because she was taken out of Man.' Therefore a man shall leave his father and his mother and hold fast to his wife, and they shall become one flesh." (Genesis 1:23-24)

[15] See John 2:1-11 for the story of Jesus' participation in a wedding in Cana, and the performance of his first public miracle.

[16] The chapter in which married women are exhorted to submit to their husbands begins here: "Therefore be imitators of God, as beloved children. And walk in love, as Christ loved us and gave himself up for us, a fragrant offering and sacrifice to God." This is an exhortation to the congregation – men and women alike. (Ephesians 5:1). These words provide the immediate context:

> And do not get drunk with wine, for that is debauchery, but be filled with the Spirit, addressing one another in psalms and hymns and spiritual songs, singing and making melody to the Lord with your heart, giving thanks always and for everything to God the Father in the name of our Lord Jesus Christ, submitting to one another out of reverence for Christ. (Ephesians 5:18-21)

In the original Greek, these verses, and the verses that follow, form one long, complex sentence.

[17] Sadly, there are many who use the text in Ephesians 5 to establish a hierarchy in marriage, with husbands lording it over their wives. There is only one Lord, and he did not marry. Mutual submission is nuanced differently for husbands and wives, but it should never be implemented in a way that undoes the mutuality and Christ-centeredness of their humility before each other. Both embrace the heart of *agape*: "My Life For Yours." Thomas Howard, *Hallowed be This House* (San Francisco: Ignatius Press, 1989), p. 47.

In my view, the nuanced mutual submission taught by the apostle Paul is best understood as preference and deference. A husband is called, in sacrificial love, to give preference to his wife, putting her interests before his own. A wife is called to give loving deference to her husband, putting his interests before her own. It is an expression of mutual honor: "Love one another with brotherly affection. Outdo one another in showing honor." (Romans 12:10) Anything other than this, anything less than this, falls short of what God intends for this relationship.

There is an analogous love between God the Father and God the Son. There is no lesser Person in the Trinity. They are equal in dignity and status, but their love is nuanced. The Father honors the Son with a preferential love (Luke 9:35; 1 Peter 1:20, NIV). The Son honors the Father with a deferential love (John 8:29; 15:10; Mark 14:36). A healthy marriage displays this facet of the *imago Dei*.

[18] Jonathan Edwards, "The Church's Marriage to Her Sons and to Her God" in *The Works of Jonathan Edwards* (Philadelphia: The Banner of Truth Trust, 1986, Vol. II, pp. 21-22.

[19] There is a difference between seeing marriage as sacramental, and regarding it as a sacrament. Protestants (myself included) are willing to affirm the first; Roman Catholics affirm the second. Catholic Christians understand a sacrament not only as a sign and tool of grace, but a conduit of saving grace: God imparts redemptive grace to sinners by virtue of receiving the sacrament. Respectfully, I believe that the Scriptures teach the first but not the second.

[20] The English word mystery in this text translates the Greek word *mysterion*, which is translated into Latin by the word *sacramentum*. I am not teaching or otherwise affirming the Roman Catholic doctrine that marriage is a sacrament.

CHAPTER 3: EDEN AND MORE!

[1] 1 Corinthians 7:17.

[2] Our word "calling" comes from the Greek, *kaleo*. Its Latin equivalent is *vocare*, from which we get the word" vocation."

[3] Quoted by Gene Edward Veith at:
http://www.modernreformation.org/default.php?page=articledisplay&var1=ArtRead&var2=881.

Gustaf Wingren comments on Luther's view:

> Vocations differ from us: farmers, fishers, and man of all orders, who handle creation's wares, carry God's gifts to their neighbors . . . . God is active in this. There is a direct connection between God's work in creation and his work in these offices. Silver and gold in the earth, growth in the creatures of the forests, the fruitfulness and unquenchable generosity of the soil, all is the ceaseless work of the God of creation, which goes forward through the labors of mankind. God creates the babes in the mother's body – man being only an instrument in God's hand – and then he sustains them with his gifts, brought to the children through the labors of father and mother in their parental office.

Gustaf Wingren, *Luther on Vocation*, trans. Carl C. Rasmussen (Philadelphia: Muhlenburg Press, 1957), p. 9.

[4] Quoted in Darby Kathleen Ray, *Working* (Minneapolis: Fortress Press, 2011) p. 74.

[5] Robert Kolb and Timothy J. Wenger eds. *The Book of Concord: The Confessions of the Evangelical Lutheran Church*, trans. Charles Arand, et al (Minneapolis: Fortress Press, 2000), pp. 400-401.

6   Paul says that a husband is the "head" of a wife, as Christ is the head of the Church (Ephesians 5:22-24). It seems significant to me that husbands are not addressed in the matter of headship. Wives are. Headship is never something that husbands are told to assert or demand, and never something that gives them permission to insist on their will in marriage. Like respect (Ephesians 5:33), headship is meaningful only if it is a gift freely and lovingly given by a wife, motivated by her reverence for Christ.

In my understanding of a husband's headship in marriage (its sole context), it is not about the rule of a husband over his wife. It is not about authority, but leadership shaped by sacrificial love and a servant's heart – both of which characterized Christ whom they follow. There is a significant difference between a ruler and a leader. Husbands are called to be the latter, but are not authorized by God to be the former. (In the one passage in which husbands and fathers are instructed to "manage" their household, submission is directed to children, not to wives. See 1 Timothy 3:1-5)

For Jesus, a leader serves by leading, and leads by serving. We see this in his characterization of himself as the Good Shepherd:

> The sheep hear his voice, and he calls his own sheep by name and leads them out. When he has brought out all his own, he goes before them, and the sheep follow him, for they know his voice.
>
> I am the good shepherd. The good shepherd lays down his life for the sheep. (John 10:3-4, 11)

A shepherd leads and lays down his life. Husbands are called to follow Christ in this. Leadership is not about a chain of command, but initiative and influence shaped by a servant's heart. Only this has transformative power for marriages, families, and our world.

7   Inspired by Thomas Howard, *Hallowed be This House* (San Francisco: Ignatius Press, 1989.

8   Paul contrasts this holiness in marriage and family with being "unclean," a ritual term from Jewish law. This may have been in the background of his thought here;

however, it would have had no meaning to Gentile believers in Corinth, and no significance for them with respect to Jewish law. Paul means much more by holiness than this.

[9] 1 Timothy 4:4-5

[10] Kolb and Wenger, *The Book of Concord*, p. 414.

[11] John Piper, Justin Taylor, eds., *The Supremacy of Sex in Christ* (Wheaton, Illinois: Crossway Books, 2005), p. 235.

[12] I am sometimes asked why God does not prevent evil in the world. He doesn't always, to be sure, but I think that he does. What he prevents doesn't happen, and so we are unaware of it. Nevertheless, we have all had uncanny experiences in which we are aware that a potential disaster was averted. An inner voice told us, "Stop!" or moved us in another direction, and we realize that something bad that was about to happen to us did not.

[13] Family and government have been designed to restrain evil and promote good in our fallen world. Even with its many flaws, government is better than lawless anarchy. Even in their brokenness and sin, in most cases husbands and wives, and parents and children, are better off living with each other in a marriage and family, than alone and on their own. Even with the problems that can justly be laid at the feet of families and ruling authorities, the world is a much better place than it would be without them. There are glimpses of God's goodness here. His patience. His kindness toward us.

[14] In *Path of Life* I wrote:

> But what about the happiness that many seem to experience, when the objects of their desire are good and wholesome, but are pursued and enjoyed without any acknowledgement of God? The desire for marriage is a reflection of God's design. Believers and unbelievers can find happiness there. Parents can find happiness in their children, even if they do not see them as good gifts from God.

Rick Howe, *Path of Life: Finding the Joy You've Always Longed For* (Boulder, CO: University Ministries Press, Revised Edition, 2017), p. 22.

15   "'For I hate divorce,' says the LORD the God of Israel, and covering one's garment with violence, says the LORD of hosts. So take heed to yourselves and do not be faithless." (Malachi 2:16, RSV)

16   "Truly, I say to you, all sins will be forgiven the children of man, and whatever blasphemies they utter, but whoever blasphemes against the Holy Spirit never has forgiveness, but is guilty of an eternal sin." (Mark 3:28-30)

17   I know that it may seem implausible and even unthinkable where you are right now, but in some cases a marriage can be restored even after divorce. God receives great glory when grace, mercy, and forgiveness prevail in human hearts, when relationships are restored, and we once again find joy in them.

18   Joy and grace are closely related. The Greek words for grace (*charis*) and joy (*chara*) are related to the root, *char*, which centers on the idea of well-being. In classical Greek *charis* (grace) means that which brings well-being, while *chara* (joy) refers the experience of this well-being. See "Grace, Spiritual Gifts" in *The New International Dictionary of New Testament Theology*, ed., Colin Brown (Grand Rapids: Zondervan, 1976) Vol. II, p. 115.

19   Here are the relevant passages in the New Testament on this:

> Now when Jesus had finished these sayings, he went away from Galilee and entered the region of Judea beyond the Jordan. And large crowds followed him, and he healed them there. And Pharisees came up to him and tested him by asking, "Is it lawful to divorce one's wife for any cause?" He answered, "Have you not read that he who created them from the beginning made them male and female, and said, 'Therefore a man shall leave his father and his mother and hold fast to his wife, and the two shall become one flesh'? So they are no longer two but one flesh. What therefore God has joined together, let not man separate." They said to him, "Why then did Moses command one to give a certificate of divorce and to send her away?" He said to them, "Because of your hardness of heart Moses allowed you to divorce your

wives, but from the beginning it was not so. And I say to you: whoever divorces his wife, except for sexual immorality, and marries another, commits adultery." (Matthew 19:1-9)

And he left there and went to the region of Judea and beyond the Jordan, and crowds gathered to him again. And again, as was his custom, he taught them. And Pharisees came up and in order to test him asked, "Is it lawful for a man to divorce his wife?" He answered them, "What did Moses command you?" They said, "Moses allowed a man to write a certificate of divorce and to send her away." And Jesus said to them, "Because of your hardness of heart he wrote you this commandment. But from the beginning of creation, 'God made them male and female.' 'Therefore a man shall leave his father and mother and hold fast to his wife, and the two shall become one flesh.' So they are no longer two but one flesh. What therefore God has joined together, let not man separate." And in the house the disciples asked him again about this matter. And he said to them, "Whoever divorces his wife and marries another commits adultery against her, and if she divorces her husband and marries another, she commits adultery." (Mark 10:1-12)

To the married I give this charge (not I, but the Lord): the wife should not separate from her husband (but if she does, she should remain unmarried or else be reconciled to her husband), and the husband should not divorce his wife. To the rest I say (I, not the Lord) that if any brother has a wife who is an unbeliever, and she consents to live with him, he should not divorce her. If any woman has a husband who is an unbeliever, and he consents to live with her, she should not divorce him. For the unbelieving husband is made holy because of his wife, and the unbelieving wife is made holy because of her husband. Otherwise your children would be unclean, but as it is, they are holy. But if the unbelieving partner separates, let it be so. In such cases the brother or sister is not enslaved. God has called you[b] to peace. For how do you know, wife, whether you will save your husband? Or how do you know, husband, whether you will save your wife? (1 Corinthians 7:10-16)

20   "Let marriage be held in honor among all, and let the marriage bed be undefiled, for God will judge the sexually immoral and adulterous." (Hebrews 13:4)

21   Behind the word "repentance" in the New Testament is the Greek word *metanoia* – a change of mind, heart, or purpose. Repentance is a change of mind that results in a change of direction and a change of life. It is rejecting the views of a sinful world, embracing God's perspective, and aligning your life with what God says.

22   "Restore to me the joy of your salvation,
     and uphold me with a willing spirit." (Psalm 51:12)

23   I recognize that in some cases a sexual relationship in marriage is not physically possible, or may not be as robust as might be otherwise desirable. This is especially true as age advances. Apart from these conditions, however, unless for temporary respites for the spiritual disciplines of prayer, celibacy within marriage is dysfunctional. There are unhealthy conditions involved, whether they are personal (stress, anxiety), relational (unresolved anger, self-centeredness, etc.) or theological (the error that in God's eyes abstinence is better than enjoying the pleasures of this gift). God does not call people to marriage and to celibacy at the same time!

24   1 Corinthians 7:6-7

25   Which is why Jesus taught that all who follow him must be prepared to lose these important relationships for his sake.

CHAPTER 4: LOVE'S DELIGHTS, PART 1

1   In this chapter and the next I will explore the loves *storge, philia, eros,* and *agape.* In his classic work, *The Four Loves,* C.S. Lewis charted the course for this, examining our experience of love through the lens of each of these loves. See C.S. Lewis, *The Four Loves* (San Diego, New York, London: Harcourt Brace Jovanovich Publishers, 1960).

2   "Anyone who does not love does not know God, because God is love." (1 John 4:8)

3   Josef Pieper, *About Love* (Chicago: Franciscan Herald Press, 1974), p. 71.

4   David W. Gill, *Becoming Good: Building Moral Character* (Downers Grove, Illinois: InterVarsity Press, 2000), p. 54.

5   C.S. Lewis, *The Four Loves,* p. 53. While this word is not used by writers of the New Testament, the love to which it points is described in other ways throughout the Scriptures.

6   Conversely, *storge* can exist without *philia, eros* and *agape,* but it is greatly impoverished without them. Many marriages endure on the basis of *storge* alone. Husbands and wives become comfortable living together and playing their respective familial roles. Often they have spent their love energy on their children, and have never developed the other dimensions of love. They stay together for the children, and may or may not stay together when their nest is empty. If they do, it is only because they prefer the status quo of *storge* to the alternatives. As important as this humble love is, there is so much more in God's design for marriages and families. There is much more joy to be gained!

7   C.S. Lewis, *The Four Loves,* p. 20.

8   The appropriate heart-response is thanksgiving, and treasuring his gifts with loving care. Without this love, neglect on the one hand, or abuse on the other, destroys the joy that God intends for us in these relationships. It is the waning of this love in our culture that has made the abortion industry possible. Whatever else may be

the case when the life of a little one is ended, love has grown cold. Jesus said that this would be true: "And because lawlessness will be increased, the love of many will grow cold." (Matthew 24:12)

9   C.S. Lewis, *The Four Loves*, p. 54.

10   Jesus introduced his followers to God as Abba, the intimate, endearing name of a child for her daddy. He provides, protects, and loves us with or without our merit, simply because he is our Father and we are his children. See, for example:

> And when you pray, do not heap up empty phrases as the Gentiles do, for they think that they will be heard for their many words. Do not be like them, for your Father knows what you need before you ask him. Pray then like this:
>
> > Our Father in heaven,
> > hallowed be your name.
> > Your kingdom come,
> > your will be done,
> >   on earth as it is in heaven.
> > Give us this day our daily bread,
> >
> > and forgive us our debts,
> >   as we also have forgiven our debtors.
> > And lead us not into temptation,
> >   but deliver us from evil. (Matthew 6:7-13)

> Therefore do not be anxious, saying, "What shall we eat?" or "What shall we drink?" or "What shall we wear?" For the Gentiles seek after all these things, and your heavenly Father knows that you need them all. (Matthew 6:31-32)

> What father among you, if his son asks for a fish, will instead of a fish give him a serpent; or if he asks for an egg, will give him a scorpion? If you then, who are evil, know how to give good gifts to your children, how much more will the heavenly Father give the Holy Spirit to those who ask him! (Luke 11:11-13)

God's parental love for us is portrayed with maternal images, as well, including pictures of a mother bird and even a mother bear:

> He [God] found him [Israel] in a desert land,
>   and in the howling waste of the wilderness;
> he encircled him, he cared for him,
>   he kept him as the apple of his eye.
> Like an eagle that stirs up its nest,
>   that flutters over its young,
> spreading out its wings, catching them,
>   bearing them on its pinions,
> the LORD alone guided him,
>   no foreign god was with him. (Deuteronomy 32:10-12)

> The LORD repay you for what you have done, and a full reward be given you by the LORD, the God of Israel, under whose wings you have come to take refuge!" (Ruth 2:12)
> Keep me as the apple of your eye;
>   hide me in the shadow of your wings. (Psalm 17:8)

> Be merciful to me, O God, be merciful to me,
>   for in you my soul takes refuge;
> in the shadow of your wings I will take refuge,
>   till the storms of destruction pass by. (Psalm 57:1)

> But I am the LORD your God
>   from the land of Egypt;
> you know no God but me,
>   and besides me there is no savior.
> It was I who knew you in the wilderness,
>   in the land of drought;
> but when they had grazed,
> they became full,
>   they were filled, and their heart was lifted up;
> therefore they forgot me.
> So I am to them like a lion;
>   like a leopard I will lurk beside the way.

I will fall upon them like a bear robbed of her cubs;
I will tear open their breast,
and there I will devour them like a lion,
as a wild beast would rip them open. (Hosea 13:4-8)

O Jerusalem, Jerusalem, the city that kills the prophets and stones those who are sent to it! How often would I have gathered your children together as a hen gathers her brood under her wings, and you were not willing! (Matthew 23:37)

God is also pictured as a human mother:

For a long time I have held my peace;
I have kept still and restrained myself;
now I will cry out like a woman in labor;
I will gasp and pant. (Isaiah 42:14)

Can a woman forget her nursing child,
that she should have no compassion on the son of her womb?
Even these may forget,
yet I will not forget you. (Isaiah 49:15)

As one whom his mother comforts,
so I will comfort you;
you shall be comforted in Jerusalem. (Isaiah 66:13)

11   Jesus' story is told in Luke 15:11-32.

12   "Honor your father and your mother, that your days may be long in the land that the LORD your God is giving you." (Exodus 20:12)

13   Robert Kolb and Timothy J. Wenger eds. *The Book of Concord: The Confessions of the Evangelical Lutheran Church*, trans. Charles Arand, et al (Minneapolis: Fortress Press, 2000), p. 401.

14   Luke 2:52

[15] Martin Luther, "The Christian in Society" II, in *Luther's Works*, ed. Helmut T. Lehmann (Philadelphia: Muhlenberg Press, 1962), Vol. 45, p. 46.

[16] Luther, "Sermons," *Luther's Works*, Vol. 51, p. 363.

[17] Jonathan Edwards saw the Christian family as a "little church."

> Every Christian family ought to be as it were a little church, consecrated to Christ, and wholly influenced and governed by his rules. And family education and order are some of the chief of the means of grace. If these fail, all the means of grace are like to prove ineffectual. If these are duly maintained, all the means of grace will be like to prosper and be successful.

Jonathan Edwards, *A Farewell Sermon* (Minneapolis, MN: Curiosmith, 2011), p. 56.

[18] If you can't live near family, you can still prioritize family love with reunions, holidays, and family vacations. Thankfully, in a day when families often live apart from each other, we have technologies that make digital real-time audio-visual interaction possible.

[19] C.S. Lewis, *The Four Loves*, p. 88.

[20] Ibid., pp. 98-99.

[21] The elimination of boys and girls clubs and athletic teams and gender-specific groups for men and women in the interests of "gender equality" betray either profound ignorance or monumental folly.

[22] Song of Solomon 5:16

[23] Friendship can exist between spouses when their shared interest is their children. If this is the only basis for friendship, however, their relationship can be jeopardized when their children become adults with interests, concerns and commitments of their own.

24   This doesn't mean that Christians can only befriend fellow Christians. Friendships can be based upon creation values and common pleasures with those who may not yet share an interest in Christ.

25   See, for example, Jesus' words to his followers:

> Greater love has no one than this, that someone lay down his life for his friends. (John 15:13)

> You are my friends if you do what I command you. (John 15:14)

> No longer do I call you servants, for the servant does not know what his master is doing; but I have called you friends, for all that I have heard from my Father I have made known to you. (John 15:15)

26   C.S. Lewis, *The Last Battle* (New York: Collier Books, 11th printing, 1974), p. 154.

CHAPTER 5: LOVE'S DELIGHTS, PART 2

[1]   C.S. Lewis, *The Four Loves* (San Diego, New York, London: Harcourt Brace Jovanovich Publishers, 1960), p. 131. Like *storge*, this word is not used by New Testament writers, probably, in this case, because it was too closely associated with views of sexuality that were utterly incompatible with a Christian vision of life. I include it because it helps us elucidate a biblical vision of romantic and sexual love.

[2]   I have had many occasions over the years to give counsel to young men during their university years who struggle with lust. My advice for them (which would be the same for women) encourages four movements of the heart: confession, affirmation, denial, embrace.

First, we all stumble and fall in many ways, and lust trips us up as often as anything. Let lust drive you to your knees before God's throne of grace. In that place of humility, confess your sins of lust, your need for his mercy and your complete dependence upon his gracious help. That is a healthy place for sinners to be!

Second, with thanksgiving, affirm the goodness of God's world, and the goodness of his workmanship in you, including your sexuality. Thank him for feminine beauty! If you are a woman struggling with this, thank him for masculine attractiveness! If you are married, thank God for your wife or your husband. If you hope to be married but aren't yet, thank him for the husband or wife he is preparing for you. Affirm the goodness of marriage and family in God's wise design for life.

Third, deny yourself. Sexual pleasure in God's design is always a gift to be given, not a prize to be taken. It is to be given and received only in marriage. Whether you are married or single, say "no" to any desire for "conquest," or "having" or "having your way" with someone. Whether you are married or single, say "no" to sex outside of marriage. Saying "no" to yourself also means saying "no" to putting yourself in situations in which you are exposed to lust's temptations. The apostle Paul told his young friend, Timothy, to "flee useful lusts." That includes the Internet, television, movies, books, magazines, and any settings of immodesty or impropriety. This is getting harder and harder to do in our world, but it is still essential to following Christ.

Fourth, embrace the fullness of life that God wants for you, that Christ came to secure for you, and that the Holy Spirit will empower you to have. It is the life of joy that I have tried to describe in *Path of Life* and *River of Delights*. The more you pursue joy, the less power lust will have over you (since the pleasures of lust are a cheap substitute for joy, and are only attractive to those who do not know joy and its ways).

³   C.S. Lewis, *The Four Loves*, pp. 134-135.

⁴   Pope John Paul II saw lust for one's spouse as impossible by the nature of the case. "This lustful look, if addressed to his own wife, is not adultery 'in his heart.' This is precisely because the man's interior act refers to the woman who is his wife, with regard to whom adultery cannot take place." Pope John Paul II, *The Theology of the Body: Human Love in the Divine Plan* (Boston: Pauline Books and Media, 1997), p. 107.

I agree that lust is a sin against marriage. There is a relational sin involved in looking at someone other than your spouse, and fantasizing sexual relations with him or her. That pleasure is prohibited by the Creator outside of marriage. Lust is not only a sin against the institution of marriage, however, it is a sin against your spouse if you are married, and a sin against your future spouse if you are not yet married.

This is lust, but lust is more than this. There is more than one problem with this sin.

Lust is a sin against our own bodies (in the same way that uniting with a prostitute is, according to the apostle Paul in 1 Corinthians 6:15-18). The desire for sexual pleasure in itself is good. God has made us sexual beings. In our fallen world, however, apart from God's grace to us in Christ, the desire for sexual pleasure becomes distorted, warped and twisted. We sin against our own sexuality when we seek gratification outside the context of marriage.

Further, lust is a sin against the Holy Spirit, whose presence within us makes our bodies a temple. We are called to glorify God in these temples, but sexual immorality, including lust, dishonors our divine Guest (1 Corinthians 6:18-20).

Lust is a sin against the image of God in another person: a sin against another human being by objectifying him or her, and treating him or her as a means to sexual gratification – even if it is done in the heart and not by physical touch. The victims of lust cease to be regarded as persons made in the image of God, and are reduced to sex objects. Sources of sexual stimulation. Lust is concerned with "having" or "having one's way" with another person. Lust regards another person as an object; Love regards the other as a rightful Subject. Love expresses itself within the context of an I-Thou relationship. Lust reduces the relationship to I-it. Sadly, this sinful dimension of lust can be found both within and outside of marriage.

Finally, lust is a sin against joy. It was the observation of another Roman Catholic, Thomas Aquinas, that the person who is "deprived of spiritual joy goes over to carnal pleasures." Lust is declining God's intended gift of joy, going over to his adversary's side, and plundering another person for self-gratification. It also ignores the deeper, spiritual, and sinful nature of lust as a substitute for joy. God intends something far better for us! He desires greater and greater experiences of his joy – which embraces all the healthy pleasures in life, including sex within marriage.

5   J.I. Packer summarizes patristic thought on sexual relations in marriage:

> Chrysostom had denied that Adam and Eve could have had sexual relations before the Fall; Augustine allowed that procreation was lawful, but insisted that that the passions accompanying intercourse were always sinful; Origen had inclined to the theory that had sin not entered the world the human race would have been propagated in an angelic manner, whatever that might be, rather than by sexual union; and Gregory of Nyssa was sure that Adam and Eve had been made without sexual desire, and that had there been no Fall mankind would have reproduced by means of what Leland Ryken gravely calls "some harmless mode of vegetation." The Fathers' background was the decadent Graeco-Roman culture that had systematically debased marriage and sexual relations for centuries, so perhaps, they, too, should not be blamed too much for views such as these. It is obvious, however, that so twisted a record needed to be set straight, and this the Reformers, followed by the Puritans, forthrightly did.

J.I. Packer, *A Quest for Godliness: The Puritan Vision of the Christian Life* (Wheaton, IL: Crossway Books, 1990), p. 261.

6   *The Library of Christian Classics, Volume II, Alexandrian Christianity*, trans. John Ernest Leonard Oulton and Henry Chadwick (Philadelphia: The Westminster Press, 1954), p. 67.

7   Jerome, "Against Jovinianus," 1:49, available online at: http://www.ccel.org/ccel/schaff/npnf206.vi.vi.I.html.

8   Augustine, "Marriage and Virginity" in *The Works of Saint Augustine: A Translation for the 21st Century*, ed. John E. Rotelle, trans. Ray Kearney (New York: New City Press, 1999), I/9, p. 35. Augustine wrote:

> What friend of wisdom and holy joys, who being married . . . would not prefer, if this were possible, to beget children without this lust, so that in this function of begetting offspring by the members created for this purpose should not be stimulated by the heat of lust, but should be actuated by his volition, in the same way as his other members serve him for their respective ends?

> [In Paradise before the Fall] The man, then, would have sown the seed, and the woman received it, as need required, the generative organs being moved by the will, not excited by lust.

> In such happy circumstances and general well-being we should be far from suspecting that offspring could not have been begotten without the disease of lust, but those parts, like all the rest, would be set in motion at the command of the will; and without the seductive stimulus of passion, with calmness of mind and with no corrupting integrity of the body, the husband would lie upon the bosom of his wife.

Saint Augustine, *The City of God*, trans. Marcus Dods (New York, NY: The Modern Library, 1950), pp. 464-75. In his interpretation of Genesis, he wrote:

> Why, therefore, may we not assume that the first couple before they

sinned could have given a command to their genital organs for the purpose of procreation as they did to other members which the soul is accustomed to move to perform various tasks without any trouble and without any craving for pleasure? For the almighty Creator, worthy of praise beyond all words, who is great even in the least of His works, has given to the bees the power of reproducing their young just as they produce wax and honey.

Augustine, *The Literal Meaning of Genesis*, trans. John Hammond Taylor, in *Ancient Christian Writers: The Works of the Fathers in Translation* (New York, NY/Ramsey, NJ: 1982), No. 42, Vol. II, p. 81.

[9]   Quoted in Vladimir Moss, *Eros in Orthodox Thought*, found at: http://www.romanitas.ru/eng/EROS.htm.

[10] Quoted in John Witte, Robert McCune Kingdon, *Sex, Marriage, and Family in John Calvin's Geneva: Courtship, Engagement and Marriage* (Grand Rapids: Wm. B. Eerdmans Publishing Co., 2005), p. 282.

See also John Calvin's *Sermons on the Ten Commandments*, ed. and trans. Benjamin W. Farley (Grand Rapids, MI: Baker Book House, 1980), p. 180: "When men and women keep themselves within the bounds of the fear of God and complete modesty, the [marriage] bed is honorable. . . . What the apostle calls honorable in God's sight is hardly a mere trifle. . . ."

[11] Quoted in Timothy J. Wengert, *Harvesting Martin Luther's Reflections on Theology, Ethics, and the Church* (Grand Rapids, MI: Wm. B. Eerdmans Publishing Co., 2004), p. 184.

[12] Thomas Hooker, Puritan leader and founder of the colony of Connecticut, wrote of this affection: "The man whose heart is endeared to the woman he loves, he dreams of her in the night, hath her in his eye and apprehension when he awakes, museth on her as he sits at table, walks with her when he travels and parlies with her in each place where he comes." Quoted in J.I. Packer, *A Quest for Godliness*, p. 265.

Augustine made this distinction between desire and joy: "When consent takes the form of seeking to possess the things we wish, this is called desire; and when consent takes the form of enjoying the things we wish, this is called joy." And, "The right will is, therefore, well-directed love, and the wrong will is ill-directed love. Love then, yearning to have what is loved, is desire; and having and enjoying it, is joy." Augustine, *City of God*, pp. 448-49.

13 Josef Pieper, *About Love*, trans., Richard and Clara Winston (Chicago: Franciscan Herald Press, 1974), p. 74.

14 John MacQuarrie writes, "As a relationship develops there is less awareness of giving and receiving as separate acts – gradually the giving and receiving are recognized only as part of the single act of sharing." From the article, "Blessedness" in *The Dictionary of Christian Ethics* (Philadelphia: The Westminster Press, 1967), p. 33.

15 Lewis uses this word for love more narrowly than it is used in classical Greek, or even in the Septuagint, the ancient Greek translation of the Hebrew Scriptures, where it often overlaps with other Greek words for love. His use is shaped by classical texts in the New Testament, and then shaped by Christian tradition. This is the way that I am using the word.

16 Thomas Howard, *Hallowed be This House* (San Francisco: Ignatius Press, 1989), pp. 46-47.

17 C.S. Lewis, *The Four Loves*, p. 166.

18 "Anyone who does not love does not know God, because God is love." (1 John 4:8)

19 "Every good gift and every perfect gift is from above, coming down from the Father of lights with whom there is no variation or shadow due to change." (James 1:17)

20 Acts 17:25

21 "For God so loved the world, that he gave his only Son, that whoever believes in him should not perish but have eternal life." (John 3:16)

22 "For even the Son of Man came not to be served but to serve, and to give his life as a ransom for many." (Mark 10:45)

23 See the following:

> Now this he said about the Spirit, whom those who believed in him were to receive, for as yet the Spirit had not been given, because Jesus was not yet glorified. (John 7:39)

> And we are witnesses to these things, and so is the Holy Spirit, whom God has given to those who obey him. (Acts 5:32)

> . . . and hope does not put us to shame, because God's love has been poured into our hearts through the Holy Spirit who has been given to us. (Romans 5:5)

24 See the following:

> Now we have received not the spirit of the world, but the Spirit who is from God, that we might understand the things freely given us by God. (1 Corinthians 2:12)

> To each is given the manifestation of the Spirit for the common good. (1 Corinthians 12:7)

> . . . and who has also put his seal on us and given us his Spirit in our hearts as a guarantee. (2 Corinthians 1:22)

> He who has prepared us for this very thing is God, who has given us the Spirit as a guarantee. (2 Corinthians 5:5)

25 C.S. Lewis, *The Four Loves*, p. 169.

26 The little prophetic book of Hosea tells the story of this sorrow. Like Hosea, the Lord is a faithful, loving husband to his people; like Gomer, the prostitute-wife, Israel spurned the love of God.

27 Universalism, the view that in the end God's love will triumph and that all will be reconciled with God, is as old as Origen (c. 185-254) and as recent as Rob Bell, *Love Wins: A Book About Heaven, Hell, and the Fate of Every Person Who Ever Lived*

(New York: HarperCollins, 2011). In my view this not only fails to square with the teaching of Jesus and the apostles, it misunderstands divine love and human freedom in God's redemptive plan. God allows us to say "No" to his love. If that is so, and we mortals turn out to be immortal after all, there must be a place for those who make that choice. That is hell.

28   In the place of God. Jesus is not merely speaking of his trips to Jerusalem and the times that he had grieved its spiritual condition. This is the voice of God expressing the heart of God over the centuries.

29   Matthew 23:37

30   C.S. Lewis describes the costliness of this love:

> God, who needs nothing, loves into existence wholly superfluous creatures in order that He may love and perfect them. He creates the universe, already foreseeing . . . the buzzing cloud of flies about the cross, the flayed back pressed against the uneven stake, the nails driven through the mesial nerves, the repeated incipient suffocation as the body droops, the repeated torture of back and arms as it is time after time, for breath's sake, hitched up.

C.S. Lewis, *The Four Loves*, p. 176.

31   Romans 5:6-8

32   "For Christ also suffered once for sins, the righteous for the unrighteous, that he might bring us to God." (1 Peter 3:18)

33   "But the fruit of the Spirit is love, joy, peace, patience, kindness, goodness, faithfulness, gentleness, self-control." (Galatians 5:22-23)

34   John 15:13, NIV. The Greek word for "love" used in this verse is *agape*; the word for "friends" is *philos*.

35   Song of Solomon 6:3

36   C.S. Lewis, *The Four Loves*, p. 177.

37   James E. Gilman, *Fidelity of Heart: An Ethic of Christian Virtue* (Oxford: Oxford University Press, 2001), p. 54.

38   Thomas Howard, *Hallowed be This House*, pp. 13-14.

www.ingramcontent.com/pod-product-compliance
Lightning Source LLC
Chambersburg PA
CBHW070528030426
42337CB00016B/2156